MW00934572

XRP 2034: Future Proves Past

Written by

Dr. Stanley Quincy Upjohn

Acknowledgments and Gratitude

First and foremost, I give thanks to our Lord and Savior, Jesus Christ, who renewed my mind, transformed my heart, and restored my soul. Without Him, nothing is possible.

To my mother, who taught me to see the beauty in everything, even money, by crafting intricate origami shirts from $5 and $10 bills—thank you for showing me that art exists everywhere.

A heartfelt thank you to my friends in high places who encouraged me to finally share my writings and discoveries. Your support pushed me to reveal a portion of an original document including cryptocurrency financial projection model we had created in the Quantum Thinktank back in 2012 and it allowed a final output through 2134 within an ancient Quantum Computer back in 2013. That document, titled *"XRP 2034: The Greatest Financial Reset in World History,"* became the catalyst for me to piece together this financial dystopian cyberpunk financial world. As the storm hit in 2024, preparing the world emotionally for the predicted collapse of the stock market and the U.S. Dollar, I found the courage to share this piece of the puzzle, offering peace of mind and hope for a brighter future.

And lastly, thank you to *Fight Club*, especially the ending—though, of course, we don't talk about *Fight Club*

Thank you to the real writers and artists on earth who inspired me to create and write more and think more deeply and beautifully about how to help others, even if I would need assistance in many ways due to brain damage. I still remember the day I heard **"More Was Never Enough"** for the first time in Morgan Freeman's voice saying "Money is NOT EVIL by itself, its just paper with perceived value to obtain other things we value in other ways. IF NOT MONEY – **WHAT IS EVIL YOU MAY ASK?** Evil is the unquenchable, obsessive and moral bending desire for MORE. EVIL is the bottomless, soulless and obsessive-compulsive pursuit of some pot of gold at the end of some rainbow which doesn't exist. Evil is having a price tag for your HEART and SOUL in exchange for Financial Success at ANY cost. EVIL is trying to buy happiness, again and again, until all of those fake, short lived mirages of emotions are gone. Imagine having it all — only to lose it all…you are now broke – all the money is gone, what do you have? The only solution to your madness and happiness was acquiring more. Now you have no more means to acquire fake happiness, no more means to acquire more. **SO…WHO ARE YOU NOW?** Where are all the people now who you thought were your friends while the money was flowing in? You might have lost your family, friends and mostly everyone in the world thinks you are a self centered, egotistical asshole. Why? Because of your endless pursuit for **more** clouded your mind and diverted you from your true purpose in life! Does this hit an emotional chord in you? Did it DEPRESS or SADDEN you?…I almost said GOOD, but I say this ONLY because I want you to change!!"

Trust the plan, it's God's plan.
If it looks like drought and there's no way out,
God's gonna make a way.
Jesus is the way.
Trust in Him alone for salvation.
Store up your treasure in heaven
Where it lasts forever.

Love always in Jesus' name,
"StanleyQ"

Table of Contents

Foreword by Anon+

In 2013, after one of the darkest periods of my life—losing investment properties from variable predatory loans of 2006, I received an 85-page PDF titled *"XRP: The Greatest Financial Reset in World History,"* mysteriously signed "StanleyQ" in an email forwarded to me by a former banking President from New Jersey who was mining Bitcoin in his attic since 2011. This manuscript gave me hope for a future built on justice, truth, and freedom from financial corruption. My full time work for spreading truth might have lost me everything, but like David in the cave while he was being hunted by his enemies in the bible, sometimes, God separates us apart to change us. I was so focused on spreading the gospel of Jesus and vaccine injury awareness campaigns, that I lost focus on money altogether…it was repulsive to me after learning about the corruption of the central banking world.

Now, a decade later, I stand on the edge of that vision becoming a reality. XRP is transforming economies, freeing people from the grip of the old financial order. I regret not encouraging Stanley to release these prophetic writings sooner, but the time has finally come. Better late than never.

In the darkest shadows of history, invisible hands controlled the fates of nations, steering the global financial quagmires to fill their own pockets at all cost while vengeance slowly built over centuries. But as my father would inform us of the risks related to pseudo-religions it was the Q triggered awakening that introduced tens of millions extra among us to our neo-financial International enslavement. And it was never about party lines, grabbing political power, or posturing —it has always been about freedom. They were the tools of freedom that we could free ourselves from control, lies, the actual very forces that have wanted to enslave humanity!

As I, too, had to step into the shadows — protecting the legacy left by my beloved Dad, and preparing for the right moment to return — I found solace in the knowledge that a **new system** was being developed.

A system that could not be corrupted, hacked, or controlled by centralized powers. That system was the **Quantum Financial System (QFS)**, and at its heart, **XRP and Ripple**.

What started as a simple digital currency soon became the **foundation for a global financial reset**, capable of freeing billions from the tyranny of debt. This is a story of how the **Quantum Financial System** saved not only our economy but our very way of life. Through XRP, we saw the **tokenization of assets** and the **rebuilding of global trust** — no longer bound by the deceit of fiat currencies or corrupt banks.

You'll read on these pages about the visionaries who made it possible, from Charlie Ward, who's passion for quantum technology led to our financial renaissance to President Donald Trump, who despite all efforts to discredit him managed to hold his ground and drain the swamp and to Elon Musk who's freedom of speech movement and exposure of lies led us into the restoration of the Republic and looking beyond the stars for the future of secure communications and banking. They all recognized XRP's long-term potential, seeing it not just as a currency, but as a tool for freedom and the foundation of a reimagined future.

The future, as you will see, has always been into the past. This is why "future proves past" — for thousands of years the financial conspiracy we are revealing today has been burrowing away behind appearances, but now it lies in tatters. What used to be Nesara then Gesara, and was merely a pipedream has now become real — implemented in conjunction with asset based digital gold standard blockchain transparency. The QFS and XRP came to us in our darkest hour and took us out of the dark ages into abundance and peace.

As you turn the pages of this book, remember to also note that if any part of this story were different, it would not just be XRP. It is the story of us all. Where we go one, we go all. While the battle for freedom is far from over, today we finally have the ability to win. This is our new beginning.

We will build a future together that no one can take away our freedom, our wealth or spirit. These few words had their beginning with a mindset — that we can do all things through Christ who strengthens us.

Welcome to the future.

— Anon+

P.S. Join us on this futuristic adventure, a quest if you will, of a lifetime. As of the date of final draft sent to publishers, **XRP price has risen 8,865% since its launch in 2013.**

Prologue: The Ripple Effect

In 2025, a historic ruling shook up the cryptocurrency universe. Ripple Labs, embroiled in a long-standing legal battle with the U.S. Securities and Exchange Commission (SEC), emerged victorious when the court ruled that XRP was not a security. The lawsuit had cast a shadow over Ripple and the broader cryptocurrency space since 2020, was resolved in Ripple's favor, setting the stage for an unprecedented surge in both the legitimacy of XRP and the entire digital asset space.

The SEC had accused Ripple of selling XRP as an unregistered security, and faced significant backlash as it became clear that this victory would reverberate throughout the financial world. The court found that Ripple's token, XRP, was legally tradable and **did not meet the requirements** to be classified as a security under the Howey Test. It was a landmark moment—one that not only vindicated Ripple but also paved the way for the entire cryptocurrency industry to flourish.

The SEC, after considering an appeal, chose not to contest the ruling. This decision sent shockwaves across the market. Overnight, XRP soared, and a new chapter in the crypto world began. The long-awaited **bull run** of XRP and its counterparts kicked off, marking the beginning of a new financial paradigm. What had started as a legal battle transformed into the dawn of a **crypto renaissance**.

Within weeks of the case settlement, another monumental event took place—the launch of **RLUSD**, a digital reserve currency fully backed by assets on the **XRPL (XRP Ledger)** and the decoupling and delisting of non-compliant digital currencies, **USDC and USDT**. Trillions of dollars from global institutions, governments, and individual investors flowed onto the ledger, catapulting XRP's market cap to unimaginable heights. The world's largest banks and financial institutions began tokenizing real estate, commodities, and even national currencies onto the blockchain. It was a global migration into the **Quantum Financial System (QFS)**, fueled by the unstoppable

1

momentum of Ripple's victory and the undeniable strength of **XRP** as a global currency.

As XRP's value skyrocketed, climbing past **$12,500 per token**, the broader financial markets began to take notice. This wasn't just a bull run—it was the **start of the greatest financial reset in world history**. The collapse of the U.S. dollar, Euro and Japanese Yen, already foreshadowed by years of unsustainable debt and inflation, was hastened by the growing adoption of XRP and the QFS. Governments and corporations scrambled to reposition themselves, aware that the old systems were no longer viable or sustainable.

This victory in the courts is the **turning point**—not only for Ripple but for the entire global financial system. The ruling signals the end of the traditional financial order, marking the beginning of **a new era** of decentralized finance powered by blockchain and cryptocurrency. It also triggers the mass adoption of **RLUSD**, the blockchain-based digital reserve currency that underpins the new global financial system replacing USDT and USDC or other non-compliant stablecoins.

The interconnectedness of world events, from the **Brunson case** wiping out Congress to the collapse of the USD and the rise of XRP. The **Ripple-SEC ruling** acts as a catalyst for the mass tokenization of assets worldwide including debt tokenization, which allowed the United States to pay back its $34 trillion debt, once and for all. Every real-world asset—whether physical, digital, or financial—is now traded on the **XRPL**, creating an **unstoppable tidal wave** of liquidity, growth, and financial freedom.

This historic settlement is going to go down in the history books as just one more way Ripple pushed back against unstable and non-asset backed financial systems, corrupt governments, and looming global conflict. It is a story not just of monetary deliverance, but also the awakening to corruption over the entire globe during tribunals. As world powers crumble and alliances change, the QFS along side XRP provides humanity with an escape pod to safety from the destruction on course of the old financial system.

Ripple's win against the SEC is more than an ordinary lawsuit victory, it represents a signal of decentralization of power and seeds sown for our future generation. As the Brunson case rips its way through Washington, breaking all of the old political and financial monopolistic regimes worldwide, dismantling the old guard, XRP's victory becomes the signal that the **Quantum Financial System**—the financial structure of the future—is already here.

Part I

The Collapse of the Old Financial World

The Collapse of the USD – 2025

I t was late Fall of 2024, and the air was thick with the tension of an impending collapse. Multiple assassination attempts, election interference and worldwide disasters including hurricanes, earthquakes, massive flooding, weaponized pathogens and wars and rumors of wars were rampant. It was the worst of times, as the world and a majority of it's population, distracted with social media and overly entertained, mainstream media controlled and manipulated were seemingly in a zombified state of complacency, like mind controlled lemmings headed toward their spiritual and financial destruction and they don't have a clue. Let me cut to the chase: the U.S. dollar is called fiat because it's fake, it's already dead. The U.S. stock market, once a symbol of global financial dominance, was teetering on the edge of ruin, bloated beyond measure with a chance for a crash so massive, it would dwarf the 1929 stock crash in one bronzing hour in the first quarter of 2025. Central banks had propped up the system for decades, printing money to maintain the illusion of stability, but the facade was starting to crack. Inflation was out of control, debt was at unsustainable levels, and faith in fiat currency was eroding fast. For years, experts had warned that the financial system was a house of cards, and now it was about to come crashing down.

In the wake of the **Brunson case**, nearly the entire Congress had been wiped out. The legal victory had stunned the nation, exposing the deep corruption within the U.S. government. Congress, it turned out, had failed to properly investigate the fraud allegations surrounding the 2020 presidential election. As a result, the judiciary had intervened, disbanding large portions of the government and leaving the country in a state of political disarray. The streets of Washington, D.C., were filled with chaos, protests, some violence and confusion as the power vacuum left by the purge began to take its toll on the population in disarray, many of which had lost everything financially. Could you imagine working a lifetime, saving for retirement and one day, it's all worth nothing?

Meanwhile, a new financial era was on the horizon. In the background, outside the crumbling walls of traditional finance, **Ripple Labs** had won a historic court case against the **Securities and Exchange Commission (SEC)**. After years of legal battles, the court had ruled in Ripple's favor, officially declaring **XRP** as *not* a security. The ruling was monumental—it was the first major court decision to acknowledge that cryptocurrencies, especially XRP, could be traded legally without being subject to the strict regulations imposed on securities.

The SEC, despite its earlier threatens of punishment, has declined to appeal after numerous court losses and appeal losses. The message that the widespread financial community took away was no screaming from the gallows of Washington DC: traditional finance is dead. A positive ruling on the legal standing of XRP has brought a massive inflow to the world crypto market, launching what appears to be an expected technical bullish cycle, the bull run of bull runs which creates more millionaires and billionaires than ever before in world history. XRP experienced a major surge in value, shooting to heights that all but the most optimistic of analysts had forecast. The bull run was not only exclusive to XRP—it had concurrently burst across the entirety of the cryptocurrency realm, especially with ISO 20022 compliant cryptos; investors and institutions, terrified fiat money would implode raced around haphazardly purchasing all crypto assets they could get their grubby hands on. In all realty, it was the Exchange-traded funds (ETFs), SEC-registered investment companies that offer investors a way to pool their money in a fund investing in stocks or bonds or other assets as Bitcoin and Ethereum did end up saving much of the wealth of retired

Americans anyways after their wise managers funnel mostly all but crashing stock selloff off into all available ETFs on Wall Street.

But XRP was different. This was more than just another cryptocurrency garnishing the wake of speculation, it served as the foundation to something much larger — The Quantum Financial System (QFS). While the rest of FinTech was lost in a sea of gloomy unknowns, they had spent years laying down what now read like a blueprint for an entirely new financial order: one that was safe from fraud and corruption; impossible to forge or fudge. And a little-known blockchain called the XRP Ledger (XRPL), which had been chugging along in near obscurity, was suddenly on course to underpin commerce worldwide.

Within weeks of Ripple's court victory, the launch of **RLUSD**, the **tokenized reserve currency** backed by real assets on the **XRPL**, sent trillions of dollars flooding into the system. The mass tokenization of everything from real estate to precious metals had begun, and for the first time, the world saw the potential of a truly decentralized financial system. Entire nations, including China and Russia, began moving their reserves onto the XRPL, seeing it as a way to escape the imminent collapse of the U.S. dollar. The global financial landscape was shifting, and XRP was at the center of it all.

As the **BRICS nations** rallied together, preparing to challenge the West, tensions escalated to new heights. China, Russia, and Iran formed a powerful coalition, with **BRICS** backing their moves to establish a new financial order based on their emerging currencies, gold, and the strategic use of digital assets like XRP. In their vision, the world would no longer be dominated by the U.S. dollar, but by a new system backed by tangible assets and decentralized technologies. Their target was clear—the **United States** and its close ally, **Israel**. These two nations represented the last vestiges of the old financial system, and the BRICS nations intended to dismantle it.

The world stood at the brink of **World War III**. The Middle East was already a powder keg, with Iran leading the charge against the Western powers. Supported by China and Russia, the Muslim nations formed an unholy alliance, ready to unleash a war of unprecedented scale. But this war was not just geopolitical—it was **spiritual**. For many, this conflict was the fulfillment of **Biblical prophecy**. The **Holy Bible** had long foretold of a time when nations would rise against each other, and only those who stood with God would prevail.

In this turbulent landscape, there were those who had been working behind the scenes for decades, anticipating this very moment. President **Donald John Trump**, under the military alliance codename **Q+**, had spent years gathering a group of loyalists, insiders, and patriots who were prepared to fight back against the global elites who had controlled the world for so long. By his side was **John F. Kennedy Jr.**, once presumed dead but now very much alive, working in the shadows to help restore the Republic and guide the people through the storm ahead. Together, they had orchestrated the **Quantum Financial System** to ensure that when the old system collapsed, the new one would be ready to take its place, at the **flick of a switch**.

One of the key architects of this grand design was **Dr. Stanley Q. Upjohn**, inspired by Charlie Ward, a brilliant but enigmatic financial theorist, programmer and early adopter of Bitcoin and Ethereum mining, who had spent his life studying the flaws in the traditional financial system and developing alternatives. Upjohn, who had been instrumental in creating the **tokenization system** that underpinned the **XRPL**, was now working with Trump, JFK Jr., and others to guide humanity through the greatest financial reset in history. His predictions, once dismissed as fantasy, were now coming true with eerie precision.

Q is the one who came up with Future proves past. The old financial system collapsed, and the Quantum Financial System rose from its ashes to show individuals that a grand plan, deemed as conspiracy theory, was now the reality. The alarm bells of quantitative easing coupled with bubbles in the stock and housing markets had been sounding for years and few bothered to listen. And while Ripple tried to scale early as their product took off and XRP shot up well beyond $12,500 a coin — soon after the tokenization of assets became global news – it was clear that Upjohn's vision had come true.

But this new world was not without its dangers. The collapse of the U.S. dollar had created a power vacuum that the BRICS nations were eager to fill. While XRP and the **QFS** offered a path to stability, the looming threat of war and the potential for global conflict hung over the world like a dark cloud.

Standing at a pivotal moment in time, with an outdated system fading away and a new one emerging—the path forward is filled with uncertainty and challenges. The **Quantum Financial System** and XRP may offer humanity a way out of the darkness, but only time will tell if they can survive the chaos that is about to engulf the globe. The battle for the future has just begun, and as Upjohn had predicted in his 2023 painting, "The Great Reset", **the ripple effect** was now unstoppable.

2

The Quantum Financial System (QFS) and XRP's Role

As the old world order of fiat and debt backed currencies disintegrated, it became clear that a new system had to emerge to restore global financial stability. This system was the Quantum Financial System (QFS), a decentralized, blockchain-based infrastructure designed to replace the legacy financial models built on fiat currency manipulation, corruption, and centralization. At the heart of the QFS was XRP, the digital asset developed by Ripple Labs, which acted as the "gas" for every transaction in this new ecosystem.

The QFS offered transparency, security, and real-time transaction processing—qualities that the crumbling fiat system had sorely lacked. The era of financial non-transparency was over. The collapse of the U.S. dollar and other major currencies created a vacuum, one that XRP and the QFS were perfectly positioned to fill. The technological advancements that made the QFS a reality, focusing on the unique role that XRP played in anchoring this revolutionary financial system.

The Need for a Quantum Financial System

The idea of the Quantum Financial System had been circulating for years before the collapse of fiat currencies in 2025. It was born out of necessity, a response to the growing dysfunction of the global financial infrastructure. Traditional banking systems, reliant on central banks, had become riddled with corruption, inefficiency, and a lack of transparency. As the digital economy expanded, the old systems proved incapable of handling the volume, speed, and security requirements of a globalized, technologically-driven world.

The QFS was designed to solve these issues by leveraging the power of quantum computing and blockchain technology. Quantum computing brought unprecedented processing power, enabling the QFS to handle real-time global transactions with complete transparency and security. At its core, the QFS was based on a decentralized ledger system that allowed for transactions to be recorded and verified without the need for third-party intermediaries like banks.

Charlie Ward and the Leadership of QFS

Charlie Ward, a well-known advocate of financial reform and a leading figure in the alternative media, became one of the key leaders driving the implementation of the Quantum Financial System. Ward, along with other thought leaders, had been outspoken about the need for a complete overhaul of the corrupt central banking system. In the wake of the USD and U.S. stock market collapse, Ward's leadership and vision were instrumental in guiding the transition to the QFS.

Ward's philosophy was simple: trust and transparency. He envisioned a world where financial transactions could no longer be manipulated by hidden actors or controlled by centralized powers. In his view, the QFS would not only restore financial balance but also enable global prosperity by eliminating the barriers that had kept billions of people in financial bondage. The QFS would be the great equalizer, and XRP would be its engine.

XRP: The Gas Token for the QFS

At the center of the Quantum Financial System was XRP, the digital asset developed by Ripple Labs. XRP was uniquely suited to act as the "gas" for the QFS due to its speed of transactions, security, and efficiency. Traditional financial systems often required several intermediaries to process cross-border transactions previously with Swift and ACH, resulting in high fees for senders and unnecessary fees to receivers plus lengthy delays as long as 5-7 business days. XRP's consensus algorithm allowed for transactions to be completed in a matter of seconds, at a fraction of the cost of traditional antiquated systems.

XRP was exceptionally valuable in the QFS because of its issued by CBDCs as bridge currencies for instantaneous liquidity between other types this Central Bank Digital Currencies, (CBDC). Brazil, Russia, India, China and South Africa had implemented their CBDCs on the XRP Ledger as well and using XRP to transfer value back-and-forth natively. XRP was the perfect asset to fuel the QFS because of its capability for instantaneous liquidity, making it able to process high volume transactions without any bottlenecks formed in traditional banking systems.

Further, since XRP serves as a gas token and nearly half of its supply was locked in liquidity pools and within individual and institutional digital wallets scattered around the world, this also effectively reduced the amount available for circulation — thus stabilizing and even increasing in price with its deflationary nature and burn-rate. The more countries and financial institutions that came into the QFS, saw XRP's market cap rocket, with it becoming within months of its creation THE dominant digital currency in this new financial world order.

Ripple Protocol Consensus Algorithm (RPCA)

What fuelled the rise of XRP and its place in QFS was mostly because of the unprecedented piece behind it i.e. The Ripple Protocol Consensus Algorithm (RPCA). Unlike other cryptocurrencies than Bitcoin which used energy-intensive PoW mechanism for transactions verification, XRP also took a break and was based on faster consensus algorithm that provided improved security with less reliance on consumption of electricity.

The RPCA, developed by Ripple Labs' chief architect David Schwartz, was designed to solve many of the problems that had plagued earlier blockchain models. In a whitepaper published in 2014, Schwartz outlined how RPCA could achieve consensus without the need for mining, significantly reducing the energy consumption and transaction costs associated with cryptocurrencies like Bitcoin.

In the RPCA, validators on the network work together to agree on the order and outcome of transactions. This process ensures that all participants in the network reach a consensus without requiring massive computational power. The RPCA's design also made it highly scalable, allowing XRP to handle thousands of transactions per second, a necessity for its role in the QFS.

At a high level, the Ripple Protocol Consensus Algorithm (RPCA) has 4 main characteristics: decentralization speed security energy efficiency. Unlike conventional systems, the RPCA uses a decentralized network of independent validators for transaction verification and thus providing increased security and resistance against attacks. The XRP Ledger transactions take 3-5 seconds to confirm, which is among the fastest compared of all other digital assets addressing immediate settlement requirement for global liquidity in synchronization with Quantum Financial System (QFS). This is also secure because the consensus model on which it operates needs a majority of validators to actually approve transactions, so no human manipulation or hacking can take place, guaranteeing transparency and trust. Moreover, the RPCA is much more energy-efficient than Bitcoin's proof-of-work model and could offer a sustainable solution for the world financial system that addresses public demand for environmentally responsible technology.

Blockchain Transparency and Accountability

Transparency and accountability was one of the main features of The Quantum Financial System. The QFS was created using blockchain tech, which allowed all transactions to be recorded on a shared ledger accessible for auditing by any party at an time. Transparency at this level was unheard of; finance is notoriously an environment for back room deals, and hidden transactions.

This made it impossible to also change or remove transactions, further helping consumers. This way, it safeguarded the implementation of fraud and manipulation as every transaction was stored eternally within blockchain ledger. This complete transparency of the QFS also held governments and financial institutions accountable for their actions like never before.

The adoption of XRP as the gas token for the QFS further enhanced this transparency. XRP's ledger was public, and anyone could verify the flow of funds in real-time. This eliminated the need for intermediaries like banks or clearinghouses, which had traditionally acted as gatekeepers in the financial system. With XRP, individuals and institutions could transact directly with one another, reducing costs and increasing efficiency.

The Integration of CBDCs into the QFS

The integration of Central Bank Digital Currencies (CBDCs) into the QFS was a crucial step in its adoption by the global financial community. The BRICS nations, which had long sought to reduce their dependence on the USD, were early adopters of the QFS and developed their own CBDCs built on the XRP Ledger. These CBDCs were designed to be stable, asset-backed currencies that could be easily exchanged for one another using XRP as the bridge currency.

The global financial system changed forever when the BRICS nations adopted the XRP Ledger (XRPL). The move towards CBDCs by different countries themselves showed that there was a necessity for interoperability — an open, secure and efficient means of transacting between various financial systems. XRP was the solution given which settles in near real-time and other than cash settlements, has large global liquidity pools.

Backed by goods like gold, oil or natural resources each CBDC had its value again unlike standard fiat currencies which do not. Its asset-backed concept, combined with the open transparency layer in XRP Ledger enabled a robust and scalable financial system that was fraud-free and not subject to inflation.

The Future of the QFS and XRP's Dominance

XRP became an invaluable element within the expanding new global Quantum Financial System. Moreover, fiat currencies were crashing worldwide and there was need of a stable currency which would be safe enough for world trade and ultimately XRP stood the best chance to serve in that capacity. Every transaction on the QFS would need XRP as their gas token, so that by every single trade transacted more and more of its use started to lock into liquidity pools and digital wallets creating reduced circulating supply increasing scarcity and value.

This QFS was more than a simply financial system; it provided an evolution of trade across the globe, allowing for none to create unscrupulous systems that worked only against nations seeking truth and stability in their economies. This demonstrated the foresight of its creators by ensuring XRP dominance within this system which was also a reflection on how far technology had come that RippleNet payments could now be possible.

The future of the QFS and XRP was bright, as more nations and financial institutions adopted the system. The world had finally moved beyond the limitations of fiat currencies and central banks, embracing a transparent, secure, and decentralized financial order powered by XRP.

3

The Fall of Central Banks

2025 brought an unthinkable event to the world financial market. Central banks, the bedrock of global economic stability were proven to be crooks and incompetents and with live tribunals broadcast worldwide, the whole world found out simultaneously. The USD collapsed under the weight of its own systemic corruption, and then appeared this economic knight in shining armor called the Quantum Financial System (QFS). During this massive transformation, XRP emerged as the world's transnational liquidity commander as we left fiat currencies forever for decentralized and blockchain-based sovereign money.

Central Banks: Destruction of the Old Guard

Central banks had nurtured the financial system globally since inception and they were effectively gatekeepers, setting policy rates, interest rates as well as practices of liquidity management to guide economies back into growth. Chief among these was the Federal Reserve, America's national bank however secretly and privately owned . The U.S. Fed was created by Congress in 1913 to promote two goals: Stable prices and maximum sustainable employment, achieved by keeping inflation and interest rates low when the economy is growing too fast, or cutting them when economic activity slows down aggressively.

But it hid many fissures beneath the facade long before that happened. The central banks had become addicted to tactics such as Quantitative Easing (QE) in which billions of freshly printed dollars were being dumped into the economy, creating asset bubbles while degrading national currencies and purchasing power. During QE, the Fed spent hundreds of billions even trillions buying in large-scale securities to push rates down and stimulate consumption. But this led to a great deal of debt that countries are still trying to repay, or unable to do so sustainably.

The Federal Reserve, along with other central banks, acted as private institutions despite claims to be publicly accountable. The blending of private and governmental characteristics, seen in the structure of the 12 Reserve Banks, was now being unveiled as a massive fraud, benefitting an elite few while destabilizing economies globally. The public began questioning how entities that were supposed to serve the interests of nations could operate with little to no transparency.

The catalyst for the fall of central banks began with the exposure of the **Federal Reserve's role in rigging interest rates** and engaging in hidden financial schemes that disproportionately affected the middle and lower classes. Hidden from public scrutiny for years, revelations surfaced of central banks manipulating interest rates for private gain, in tandem with large financial institutions. This triggered distrust not only in the U.S. but worldwide, as central banks everywhere faced similar accusations. As central bank failures reached a peak, a warning from the Q team echoed in the background and on the 4-chan and 8-chan boards: **"Follow the money."**

XRP and the Quantum Financial System (QFS)

Amidst waning trust in traditional finance, the Quantum Financial System (QFS) materialized and challenged nearly everything we thought possible. The QFS had been designed as a fool-proof and fraud-free with full transparency on any financial transaction. Underpinned by XRP, this served as an entirely new international financial system far removed from the fiat-based central bank-controlled monetary paradigm.

Several benefits over the old economic system were made available by The Quantum Financial System (QFS). It solved this problem by using a public ledger to record every transaction so financial activity could be recorded and monitored. Security-wise, QFS technology used the most advanced quantum computing methodology so it was practically impossible to hack and manipulate. Secondly, speed was a dominant trait as well since the ability of XRP to execute lightning fast transactions soon became possible utilizing its underlying protocol: The Ripple Consensus Algorithm which made it superior in global cross border payments.

XRP was that much of a perfect fit because its own consensus algorithm is different from traditional mining as we have seen on other digital assets. While Bitcoin utilizes a proof-of-work system, XRP was developed as an energy-efficient solution for handling thousands of transactions per second with no third party when David Schwartz released his whitepaper on Ripple's Protocol Consensus Algorithm.

Under the QFS, XRP became the world's de facto liquidity provider. Governments and banks began to lock XRP into their digital wallets for every transaction, reducing the circulating supply and driving its value skyward. The shift was instantaneous: as the USD lost its status as the world's reserve currency, **XRP** surged to unimaginable heights.

BRICS and the Rise of Central Bank Digital Currencies (CBDCs)

A major player in this financial reset was the **BRICS nations—**Brazil, Russia, India, China, and South Africa. These nations had long sought to establish a financial system independent of the Western-dominated SWIFT network and the USD. In the years leading up to 2025, they developed their own **Central Bank Digital Currencies (CBDCs)**.

BRICS' **CBDCs** were secretly built on the **XRPL (XRP Ledger)**, integrating seamlessly into the QFS. As these nations moved their economies onto this decentralized system, the demand for XRP as the gas token for all transactions skyrocketed. By **locking billions of XRP tokens** into their national digital wallets, they effectively took these tokens out of circulation, increasing scarcity and driving up XRP's value further.

This strategic alignment with the QFS allowed BRICS nations to challenge the economic dominance of the West, while securing their financial systems through blockchain technology. As their influence grew, other countries began to follow suit, shifting their economies from central bank-controlled fiat to decentralized digital currencies powered by XRP.

Nesara-Gesara Reforms and XRP's Ascension

Meanwhile, there is a start of the implementation by soon worldwide of Nesara-Gesara reforms that for so long was mentioned only as being fringe conspiracy theories. The underlying goal of these worldwide financial reforms, was to restore world wealth and take down national debts, cancel income tax as we know it today globally and unleash suppressed technologies and financial prosperity tools directly to "we the people".

The QFS, anchored by XRP, was the vehicle through which these reforms were implemented. As old financial systems collapsed, XRP became the global standard of value. Every nation, now free from the control of central banks, adopted XRP to conduct trade and stabilize their economies. The currency wars of the past were over; XRP, through its integration into the QFS, united the world under a single, transparent system.

The End of Central Banks

In 2025, there were no longer central banks. The days of hidden financial manipulation were gone, and a new era in decentralized finance was born. The flywheel of monetary inflation, bailouts and corruption that fed the old system was gone — replaced by a fully transparent network where all assets were tokenized and every trade encrypted on-chain ensuring everyone could verify any transaction and wallets in real time on the XRPL.

With central banks collapsing and XRP at the fulcrum of a fledgling QFS, it was the birthmark of a new global financial age that signalized transparency, stability and an era in which everybody wins.

With the introduction of QFS and the power of blockchain technology, central banks were naturally overthrown by their corruption and manipulation in broad daylight on a global scale. The growth of XRP, on a worldwide scale will be seen as more than just another technological breakthrough; throughout history it would be celebrated as the second financial revolution: liberation from national currencies and monopoly central banks. The world was a different place, that could never be denied. The future proved the past.

4

Sealed Indictments and Financial Crimes Exposed

The shockwaves went around the world the moment 400,000 sealed indictments began leaking out when taking down various industry titans as the first 40,000 indictments have morphed into citizens yelling for justice. Such indictments began revealing how a gigantic international web of financial corruption, insider trading, money laundering and price-fixing had been operating in the darkness for generations. Previously institutions were found to be culpable in massive abuses and fraud, with systemic changes needed — a financial revolution. The global economic system that the people were familiar with was in decay and resistance to its reinvention, a transformation enforced by XRP & Quantum Financial System (QFS) led.

These indictments are at a staggering level. Never before in history have we seen such a concerted plan to disrupt old legacy systems of lies and corruption. However, this Operation by military intelligence and international partnership thereof is now evident to your global audience of those sealed indictments across governments & corporations including the powerful elite signifies a world wide movement for the betterment — to protect humanity and liberate all from current societal constrains. And now, as the indictments are unsealed, we are witnessing The Storm — a worldwide military intelligence operation to bring law and order back to society.

Insider Trading and Market Manipulation

At the heart of these indictments lies the pervasive issue of **insider trading** and **market manipulation**, which have eroded the trust and integrity of financial markets worldwide. Prominent political figures, corporate executives, and influential investors are among the main perpetrators of these crimes. One notorious example is **Rep. Nancy Pelosi** and her husband, **Paul Pelosi**, who have long been accused of profiting from insider information. In 2023, the Pelosis invested millions in **NVIDIA (NVDA)**, a tech giant set to benefit from the **CHIPS and Science Act**, which Nancy Pelosi supported. Their trades, conveniently timed around legislative developments, resulted in substantial gains, prompting public outcry and legislative proposals like the **PELOSI Act**, which seeks to ban members of Congress from trading stocks altogether.

Such actions highlight the deep rot within the financial system, where those in power manipulate the system for personal gain while hardworking citizens suffer the consequences. The unsealed indictments reveal that numerous high-ranking corporate officials have been exploiting their access to privileged information, manipulating stock prices to maximize their personal wealth. This rampant manipulation has created shockwaves throughout the global economy, destabilizing markets and undermining public trust.

Corporate Collusion and Price Fixing

Corrupting a corporation — The indictments also revealed corporate mega-collusion and price fixing. It is the same kind of anti-consumer charade that has generated so many headlines in recent months and years, from pharmaceuticals to energy. These conspiracies have permitted multinational corporations to preserve their dominance, obviously restricting the entry of newcomers and inflicting high prices on consumers.

The pharmaceutical industry has been a main target of these indictments. Even established drugmakers, such as Teva Pharmaceuticals and Glenmark Pharmaceuticals have been found to be in an illegal collusion for hiking prices of important drugs like those used for high cholesterol and cystic fibrosis. Teva ultimately reached a settlement with the companies in 2023, agreeing to pay $225 million. Pfizer was also caught colluding with Mylan to charge six times the normal price of EpiPens ($100 rising to $600 per pen over only a few years), showing just how widespread pharmaceutical corruption really is.

Companies like Western States Petroleum Association (WSPA) and Energy Transfer Partners have also been at the forefront of corruption in energy, with accusations ranging from allocation-based pricing to market manipulation. The prices in these cases are prime examples of corporate greed seeping into core sectors and sparking outrage.

TD Bank's Role in Financial Crimes: A Historic Reckoning

One of the biggest bomb shells regarding sealed indictments is how they link to major financial institutions in terms of criminal activities. TD Bank, one of North America's largest banks and a decade-old money laundromat that led to this week's historic $3 billion settlement with the U.S. Department of Justice. TD Bank, one of the worlds largest banks, and its actions related to todays announcement were designed to warn other entities that it could not flout international laws with immunity when they hampered criminal activity.

According to Attorney General Merrick Garland, TD Bank's lax practices allowed a wide range of illicit activities to flourish, including drug trafficking, human trafficking, terrorist financing, and fentanyl distribution. The bank's leadership was alerted to significant shortcomings in its anti-money laundering program, yet failed to act, with employees openly joking about how easy it was for criminals to launder money through TD Bank's systems. Garland stated, "By making its services convenient for criminals, TD Bank became one itself."

One egregious example involved a single individual moving over **$470 million** in drug proceeds and illicit funds through **TD Bank accounts**, bribing employees with gift cards in return for ignoring suspicious activities. In another case, **TD Bank** employees helped criminal organizations launder **$39 million** to **Colombia**, with red flags like the use of identical Venezuelan passports to open multiple accounts going unnoticed until one employee was arrested. The Justice Department's investigation is ongoing, and more **financial institutions** are expected to be implicated as these sealed indictments are unsealed.

The **TD Bank** case is just one example of how global financial institutions have been complicit in money laundering schemes that perpetuate criminal activities worldwide. The revelations from the **TD Bank** settlement serve as a stark reminder that no institution is immune to corruption, and accountability is long overdue. The **sealed indictments** provide the necessary framework for holding these institutions accountable and reforming the global financial system.

Financial Institutions and the Global Reckoning

The revelations from TD Bank were not an isolated incident. Other high-profile financial institutions, including Goldman Sachs, JPMorgan Chase, and HSBC, have been implicated in money laundering and fraudulent activities on a massive scale. For instance, HSBC, which faced previous penalties for laundering drug cartel money in Mexico, was found to have engaged in even deeper corrupt practices. JPMorgan Chase was embroiled in the London Whale scandal, which exposed its traders' risky behavior, resulting in billions of dollars in losses. These institutions, once seen as untouchable, are now under intense scrutiny as the full scope of their complicity in financial crimes comes to light.

The unsealing of these indictments reveals that financial institutions have long been enablers of **global corruption**, facilitating the movement of illicit funds and allowing criminal networks to flourish. These revelations have prompted calls for a complete overhaul of the **financial system**, with a focus on transparency, accountability, and the integration of **blockchain technology** to prevent future crimes.

Military Tribunals and Public Accountability

As the indictments are unsealed, the military's role in bringing justice becomes even more crucial. **Military tribunals** have been prepared to handle the vast scale of financial and political crimes, bypassing the **corrupt civilian court systems** that have failed to deliver justice for years. These tribunals, which will be broadcast globally, represent a pivotal moment in the fight against **financial crimes** and **government corruption**.

The military tribunals are not just about punishing the guilty—they are about restoring **public trust** and demonstrating that no one is above the law. These trials, involving some of the most powerful people in the world, will serve as a warning to those who seek to exploit the system for personal gain. The transparency of these proceedings ensures that the public can witness justice in action, holding leaders and institutions accountable for their actions.

The XRP Ledger and the Quantum Financial System: The Future of Finance

The unsealing of these **400,000+ indictments** and the exposure of corruption in the financial system has paved the way for a new era of **accountability** and **transparency**. At the center of this transformation is **XRP** and the **Quantum Financial System (QFS)**. As the corrupt financial institutions collapse, **XRP** has emerged as the cornerstone of a new, decentralized financial system.

The **XRP Ledger**, built on blockchain technology, ensures that every transaction is publicly traceable and immutable, making it impossible for criminal activities to go undetected. The **burn mechanism** of XRP, which reduces the number of tokens in circulation with every transaction, further increases its value and solidifies its role in the future of global finance. By eliminating the need for corrupt intermediaries and allowing for the free movement of assets across borders, XRP is revolutionizing the financial landscape.

Decentralization of the financial system not only has a role in combating corruption — it can help build an equitable and more transparent world where crimes such as money laundering or tax evasion no longer occur. Governments, corporations and individuals will be brought to justice as the XRP/QFS paves way for a new ecosystem of integrity, transparency & accountability.

The appearance of 400,000+ sealed indictments; the uncovering of financial crimes; and XRP & QFS implementation herald a renaissance. Governments and corporations are crumbling, the people who used to make money off of others making themselves suffer are being held accountable at last. The world is going through a global wake-up call where transparency, justice and accountability has become not an option but necessary.

The war against corruption is truly at hand and as we see the sealed indictments be unsealed, these military tribunals are now becoming front and center…the whole world watches. The financial reset is not just a monetary transition, it is spiritual and moral renewal. The ancient systems of corruption and servitude are bursting from their seams, as a new world order readies to rise in its place — one not coming into existence by way of more deception and violence but through the arms-open-wide embrace of truth. We are finally on the cusp of Republic Restoration, with XRP and QFS (Quantum Financial System) at the forefront leading us straight into a sharable accountability future where corruption will soon be extinct.

5

XRP, Tokenization, and the Future of Global Assets

Legacy banking and investment, which have been such a part of our economic lives for so long, are themselves being disrupted by both blockchain technology AND digital assets. At the forefront of this ever-expanding core is XRP: a digital asset that can bridge currencies and borders more efficiently and deliver value across them in new safer ways. One of the breakthroughs that XRP is representing open free access to any asset tokenization, which would provide a level of liquidity and transparency in global finance never seen before.

The Concept of Tokenization

Tokenization: The rights to an asset are converted on a blockchain into a digital token and the term used for this process is called Tokenization. This method will allow both real and virtual assets to be registered with a legal title as token which should be globally tradable on international markets. One of the major benefits is providing liquidity and ownership rights transfer for other types of asset, to be liquidize or proper owner registration recorded with real-estate other commodities goods like intellectual or properties. This has resulted into several middlemen adding unwanted friction in to the market. An asset is tokenized means which split in hundreds or even thousands of tiny parts, makes it more tradable to exchange and effectively split ownership between different types.

Wouldn't it be cool to own a piece of a luxury yacht, a Picasso or even commercial real estate like with Island Project? This enables ownership of such assets by tokenizing them, breaking these large into smaller tokens which represent shares in the ownership. Those tokens are then traded over a blockchain and allow for instant settlement, as well we fractional ownerships that democratize investments and project governance.

XRP, because of its quick settlement speeds and low transaction fees is turning into the perfect vehicle for tokenizing worldwide resources. The XRP Ledger (XRPL) is one of the largest decentralized platforms created for launching, circulating and documenting tokenized assets on a distributed ledger which allows permissioned participants to settle transactions.

The Rise of Tokenized Assets

With the continuous expansion of blockchain technology, industries in every corner of the world are beginning to realize what tokenization can do for them. Projects such as The Island Project from AMTV innovator Christopher Greene are at the forefront of this transition, paving ways for real estate tokenization. Flagship Project 1 of his Hawaii-based tokenization illustrates how tokenization can grant fractional ownership to luxury homes, condos, land and retreats heretofore typically inaccessible for individual investors.

The Island Project, for example uses blockchain technology to enable investors to buy Non-Fungible Parcels (NFPs), giving actual ownership in the properties within its portfolio. This is what you need to turn the real estate investment game around; prime assets in Maui and Oahu. Investors have the possibility to access a decentralized network that offers capital appreciation, income from vacation rental and unique membership privileges with only 33,500 existing units available with a three year holding period for early investors.

Not only does this tokenization model expand ownership of real estate into a new segment, it significantly decreases transaction times and increases liquidity as well. The Island Project enables immediate settlements via blockchain and reduces some of the disadvantages that are inherent in traditional forms of real estate investments.

The broader financial markets are seeing the same type of progress with tokenization introducing traditional assets like stocks, bonds and commodities. Digitalising these assets enables 24/7 trading hours and quicker settlements, radically mitigating counterparty risk. XRP provides another great example with its ledger that is both decentralized and requires no central intermediary: this shows how tokenization can be a solution for borderless, instantaneous settlement without needing expensive middlemen in between.

It is a dramatic example of its potential to disrupt not just real estate, but everyone within the entire global securities market. Platforms like the Island Project will be at the forefront of this multi-trillion dollar industry simply by uniting people in fractional ownership and enabling easy transactions through blockchain.

Global Impact on Industries

The tokenization of assets can disrupt far more than real estate and finance Tokenization is changing art and collectibles, for instance. Digitized Art, Digital Assets and Non-Fungible Tokens (NFTs) for exclusive pieces of edgy art or impossible-to-get collectibles spurs a multi-billion dollar market in digital ownership. Artists can now sell a fraction of their original works of art, to reach a broader and more efficient audience. Tokenized collectibles also provide a means for new types of investment opportunities and charitable auctions in the digital age, as is now happening with GalleryHope.com where over 50% of all revenue goes to supporting educational scholarships for families challenged with Autism.

For example, in the energy space tokenization could mean new ways of trading and owning. Tokenization would clear up a substantial aspect of the economy, in this case some renewable energy credits (RECs), which are traded with great difficulty through hardly transparent marketplaces. Energy producers and consumers could leverage Blockchain technology to create tokens for trading of renewable energy that would bring innovation an sustainability into the energy use industry.

The tokenization is aimed to be a game-changer in the market for Intellectual Property (IP) as well. Writers, musicians and other creators might be able to tokenize their creative output — i.e. sell shares in the future revenue of that effort by offering access using NFTs on a blockchain network. This could mean that artists have access to capital, while investors can tap into asset classes they might not otherwise. Combined with XRP's ability to scale and handle microtransactions, as well as royalties,it makes an excellent platform for these new IP markets.

The Role of XRP in Asset Liquidity

Liquidity is essential in financial markets. Assets lacking liquidity are hard to trade and lead to volatile markets. A big part of what makes XRP so powerful lies in the kind of liquidity improvements it can enable for a diverse set of assets.

With the tokenization of assets on the XRP Ledger, liquidity possibilities are unlocked in ways never thought before. Because of this, a tokenized asset can be bought or traded immediately and does not use traditional intermediaries such as a broker or clearinghouse. This not only fastens the settlement process, but also cuts it down on the transaction cost.

Furthermore, it can achieve its use as a bridge currency for transferring tokenized assets between chains or zones. With all these blockchain networks, there is a necessity to have a common settlement layer in this fragmented world of finance. XRP is in a unique position to help solve this problem, allowing for value to move across different blockchains and payment systems.

A real estate property token on the Ethereum blockchain, for example, could be transferred to a buyer on XRP Ledger with XRP fulfilling as cross-blockchain intermediary. This cross-chain capability further expands liquidity, and allows the asset to flow freely through networks from platform to another.

Transparency and Trust In Global Finance

Transparency is one of the biggest issues that global finance faces today. Financial markets tend to be more opaque, while intermediaries and gatekeepers hold a strong hand in controlling the circulation of information. This makes a platform where fraud, corruption and market manipulation can easily prosper.

Tokenization, especially on the XRP Ledger promotes transparency to an unparalleled level in financial markets. A full and immutable record of all activity is maintained on the blockchain for any transaction. This makes the tokenized assets traceable, auditable thereby minimizing fraud risks and providing investor assurance.

Secondly, tokenization allows access to investment opportunities for the masses. As things stand now, several asset classes are only available to wealthy individuals or institutional money. By tokenizing assets, the industry is essentially breaking them down into tiny little pieces making it more available to small time "mom and pop" investors who never had a chance at venture capital or unique real estate… until today.

Tokenization and the Future of National Currencies

With central banks across the globe considering rolling out of Central Bank Digital Currencies (CBDCs), tokenization is set to gain even greater importance. In other words, you can say CBDCs are something like the cryptographic tokens of national currencies that allows them to be seamlessly tradable on XRP or another blockchain platform. It can change how national monies are issuing, managed and transferred.

With its fast transaction times and extremely low fees, XRP is the perfect candidate for issuing and transacting CBDCs. China, Sweden and the Bahamas are among other countries that have been looking into introducing CBDCs to help usher their financial systems into a more contemporary age. Central banks can leverage blockchain technology to benefit from the transparency and security created it provides while keeping their currency liquid and transferable.

It may also help accelerate the transition of tokenized asset usage, as national currencies further embed themselves with blockchain networks. This will create a single seamless platform for both traditional and digital assets where liquidity is further increased while transaction costs are being reduced.

The Long-Term Vision: A Tokenized World

As we go forward, the asset tokenization space is poised to change not only finance but a major part of global economy as well. Over the long term, as tokenization broadens to include more types of assets barriers between markets will erode giving way to a global market even value exchange can be done in an instant and trustless manner.

XRP leads the charge into this transformation. It is opening the world to a tokenized asset society and new financial system that will work for everyone, everywhere with nothing left in between. From real estate to art, energy or even intellectual property — digital tokenization is opening up new avenues for investing and trading like never before.

Blockchain Engineering and Tokenization are the future of finance!! But XRP is no longer a cryptocurrency, and that's why it really just brings the worldwide market capitalization of cryptos even higher, bringing in trillions of dollars when tokenization of assets and backing of XRP with Gold. The innovation of this new open payments system is being built on top of XRP, and moving the world towards a future where value will no longer be confined or constrained by borders, intermediaries or outdated financial systems. Tokenization of assets is a world where everyone, everywhere has complete access to the global market and XRP is starting it all. The future will not be digital-only — It is tokenized and XRP is the gas behind this unstoppable blockchain engine.

Part II

The Financial Revolution

6

Time Travel and the Return of JFK Jr.

I t was the year 1999, and the Kennedy family, already steeped in tragedy historically with the assassinations of both John F. Kennedy and Robery F. Kennedy just a few decades before, was hit again by the presumed death of JFK Jr. That year, John F. Kennedy Jr presumably perished in a plane crash while flying his personal aircraft off the coast Martha's Vineyard. Since that day, speculation about what really happened in the cockpit and the bodies has been widely discussed and produced many conspiracy theories, but make no mistake; very few believed the official account then--and nobody believes it even now. The search for this ill-starred group of three and their remains has never ended. On the one hand they were a source of ineffable sorrow for a world that had lost one its most talented prodigal sons; on the other, however, public compassion and concern had carried them forwards time after time.

Even though the public doesn't know it, this disappearance was in fact a skillfully arranged military orchestration of intrigue as part of the largest military operation in world history. Kennedy was forewarned of the danger threatening his life and Looking Glass technology showed him one assassination scene after another, just like the one which killed his father, President John F. Kennedy, decades before.The deep state, still nervous about the legacy of the Kennedys, selected him as a target because of his investigations into hidden power structures and corruption. But with Looking Glass technology he was able to see what was going to happen and then prevent it from taking place.

33

Looking Glass: The Key to Evading Assassination

Looking Glass technology was first in the rumors of secret government projects. It has the ability to see forward into potential future outcomes. As far back as the early time looking-glass, technology was used in high military applications that allowed certain individuals a glimpse of different time streams. However, rather than just offering a peek here and there, it actively influenced events and shaped developments.

When he learned that his assassination was being planned for 1999, JFK Jr. understood that simply hiding out would not suffice. He had to disappear completely — he had to let the world see him die in order to secretly infiltrate and sabotage the very powerful forces which sought his life. The Looking Glass gave him this insight to make things work out. With the aid of trusted military colleagues and friends who were also using this technology to oppose the deep state, together with military intelligence, JFK Jr. faked the plane crash into existence with within the military are known as "White Hats". For decades he lived in the shadows, largely in disguises and using pseudonyms as advised by Looking Glass, trained up close with figures like President Donald Trump. Both Trump and JFK Jr. had a common task: to break up the entrenched powers that had been corrupting nations and economies for centuries.

The Reemergence of JFK Jr.

JFK Jr.'s return had been meticulously planned and coordinated. With the 2024 Election approaching and President Donald Trump unable to hold down the tide set in motion by people deeply embedded within government departments, it was time for JFK Jr. to re-enter the public eye. His resurrection would not be just symbolic; it was a cold calculation to restore the public's faith in truth, transparency and justice. JFK Jr. and his cousin Robert Kennedy Jr. were the inheritors of the Kennedy legacy— an unfinished fight against those who had tried to destroy their clansmen's family, now more powerful than ever before.

But his return went beyond mere family dynasties. It was about injecting the Looking Glass technology into a grander program: The Great New Financial Reset. Working alongside Trump, myself (Dr. Stanley Q. Upjohn), and Charlie Ward, JFK Jr. played a key role in the rise of the Quantum Financial System (QFS). Using XRP and its associated technologies, they planned to overthrow old fiat currency systems and a taxation without representation that funded already overused warfare, its lopsided benefits accruing for decades primarily-- without any doubt--to the benefit of only a very small clique worldwide, and replace all of these with a decentralized transparent financial ecosystem.

The Partnership with Trump

Although JFK Jr. kept a low-key existence in the shadows, he did finally realign with Trump before he famously came down the Trump Tower escalator even predicted in the Simpsons, one of JFK Jr.'s deep fake mask characters first appeared, look back at the video, Donald acknowledges me right has he proceeds to descend in the escalator. Future proves past. As both men had experienced the corruption and control of these secret cliques and global finance's power holders, they both sought justice and to restore the American Republic. Thanks to movie screen technology, Obama's spying presidency and Bush's FBI/CIA corruption coalition as well all collapsed like dominoes into waste under the Commander in Chief Trump. Look back for his executive orders, watch some of Derek Johnson's videos, he breaks it down clear as day. Their fight was far from finished, it had just begun.

Though JFK Jr. and Trump had known each other for years and both men suffered under the sway of these hidden evil forces of the world, Trump had long promised to "drain the swamp", while JFK Jr. would promise to get justice for the assassination of his dad and expose all of the corruption and hold accountable any and all governmental agencies who were complicit. Thus far they had managed to evade threats to their lives and help to save the economy, and strategies for dismantling a malign power control deep within their own American state--all thanks to the Looking Glass Software and their faith in God.

The Assassination Attempts

Trump, like JFK Jr., was the target of multiple assassination attempts, many of which were not made public due to their sensitive nature. One of the most shocking attempts took place in 2024 during a golf game, which eerily paralleled an earlier painting by Upjohn entitled "Trump and JFK Golfing", where Trump's back is facing the nature which hid his assassin. The gunman, armed with a rifle and GoPro to record is all, had ties to a financial cabal aiming to stop the Quantum Financial Reset. His left behind note was unnecessarily publicized mentioning a $150,000 bounty on Trump's head added to the danger. The media's role in circulating this information, increasing risks, may also be scrutinized for complicity in sedition and possibly treasonous acts.

JFK Jr., having used Looking Glass to foresee this attack, took preemptive steps with the aid of military intelligence. The assassination attempt failed, but it showcased how critical the fight against these forces had become. The deep state was becoming increasingly desperate as the QFS and the growing power of XRP threatened to dismantle their financial stranglehold.

The Quantum Financial System and XRP's Role

JFK Jr.'s and Trump's cooperation was not just political-they were fit partners for secure global finance free from manipulation of any kind, one that would change the financial world forever and return centuries of taxation without representation reparations for all Americans and similar nations around the world complicit in crimes against humanity.. They saw this endeavor not merely as an economic challenge but also another way to realize the ideals of a "end of FightClub" scenario metaphorically speaking of the collapse of the old financial system and rising Phoenix of the XRP blockchain powered QFS to prevent disaster and societal collapse during financial collapse   QFS, home to

International Monetary Fund currency, accounts, trading systems and money weary banks and corporations would explode in prosperity if XRP once given free reign and approval from the SEC during the 3rd term of President Trump —its function of asset tokenization in addition to providing global liquidity (Q+).

The QFS was unprecedented in many ways, namely security as nothing could be hacked or counterfeited. Transparency throughout operations and transactions at every level, from deal-making smart contracts to every piece of news would automatically go into the public realm unobscured by noise; and of course speed on the blockchain. Economic crimes could not be committed without the proper vehicles, otherwise all investigation effort would come to naught. Taking a hands-on approach with key figures like Charlie Ward, JFK Jr. pulled the strings so that QFS became the foundation of global finance, trust and security beyond reproach. Tokenization and liquidity provided by XRP allowed assets to be held a great number of times (meaning wealth was no longer in the hands of just a few). It meant that everyone could participate in wealth generation; the tokenization of everything — from real estate to all commodities and futures contract forever now on the blockchain. The old hierarchies were coming apart along the seams, as was the power of so-called deep state programs.

Nesara-Gesara Reforms: Opening to a New Era

The return of JFK Jr. also meant the implementation of Nesara and Gesara reforms was "on", finally not an empty promise or conspiracy theory of any kind! The kind of reforms that had been effectively smothered by the elites for decades, were finally becoming a reality. The QFS, Gold backed XRP and "flip of a switch" Financial Reset and a new digital currency backed by real world and digital Tokenized Assets, Debt, Power and ultimately global currency reform.

Nesara and Gesara also included debt relief along with the release of assets that were stolen from us by our government, who advises this same criminal organization in turn for a piece of their pie. Under the leadership of Charlie Ward and his supporters along with JFK Jr. and

President Trump, this was all part of Global Civil War reforms that were resetting a global landscape to return power back to people as they stripped away systems designed for them not only suppress but control.

The Endgame: Looking Glass and the Future

The entire point of the Looking Glass technology wasn't to predict what will occur but pick a future and push for it. JFK Jr and Trump used this technology successfully to go around their enemies, avoid attempts at assassination on the way... leading up to world financial reset.

With the implementation of QFS and RUBIX/XRP as well, this planet was now into a new era. The assets have been tokenized, and this type of transparency had never existed before; the economic balance has also returned thanks to Nesara-Gesara reforms.

The implications of JFK Jr returning were not just symbolic, it was a hardening point to end the Deep State and establish financial freedom. He had witnessed the outcome with Trump and their comrades by Looking Glass, just as he was making it happen.

JFK Jr.'s disappearance and return, not by chance or luck had been planned in advance. Leveraging advanced technology enabled him to stay a step ahead of those who sought to destroy him and his vision; JFK Jr.'s fate was not something determined by luck. Alongside Donald Trump, Charlie Ward, yours truly "QArtist" or "StanleyQ" (Dr. Stanley Q. Upjohn), and the military intelligence alliance helped guide the world toward a Quantum Financial System that would be backed by XRP. The power of prayer and faith broke the old corrupt order, pointing towards future transparency, prosperity and true financial freedom for all.

7

Charlie Ward's Gold Backed Quantum Financial System

It was Charlie Ward's pursuit of hidden gold supplies that significantly affected both the QFS (Quantum Financial System and XRP. For years, the world's economy had been held together through the manipulation of fiat currency systems with the resultant wealth focused in the hands of a few. Central banks, corporations and governments ruled the world money by means of debt and fiat currency manipulation, leaving little chance for ordinary people to ever accumulate real wealth, government debts approaching unpayable, like America's $34 trillion dollar debt which would be paid before the end of President Donald Trump's 3rd Term in office. The deep state, as it was known, enjoyed this centralized command-and-control for centuries, squeezing its grip on countries, governments and individuals every year. However, old systems were about to be changed forever when the QFS and revolutionaries like Ward and President Trump started coming into their own, "out of the shadows, into the light, get back up with all His might". Scripture speaks very little about money, but it seems that Gold and Silver are God's money, so we will tokenize it on the XRPL. 'The silver is Mine, and the gold is Mine,' says the LORD of hosts. 'The glory of this latter temple shall be greater than the former,' says the LORD of hosts. 'And in this place I will give peace,' says the LORD of hosts." Haggai 2:8-9 (NKJV).

For many years, Ward had been interested in the relationship between gold and fiscal value, as well as his deep Christian faith and reverence for the Bible and faith in Jesus Christ as his Lord and Savior. History showed gold to be one of the few assets which had held its value throughout the centuries. Even in times of financial crisis and stockmarket crash, its luster remained untainted. Nonetheless, by the ancient 20th century whole nations had become enamored of paper money and the gold standard was abandoned. This enabled the central banks to issue money without any backing, thereby devaluing all currencies and giving rise to wild inflation. Ward grasped this manipulation for what it was—a devious trick to enrich the few at the expense of masses. He knew that providing a stable and universally acknowledged asset to back up the QFS was paramount. The asset he chose? Gold.

For years the rumor mill turned out stories of hidden gold reserves passed on from one conspiracy theory hunter or Nesara and Gesara researcher to another. Some said that long ago in their decline an ancient civilization hid extraordinary amounts of gold, while still others believed that the modern governments and leading families owned secret vaults-filled to the brim with enormous reserves. Ward, always an investigator, pursued these tracks with dogged determination. His detective work unearthed leads that led him to documents and maps, voices from the underground financial world— all of which pointed towards hidden gold deposits comparable to any known in the world, many of which were confiscated during the largest military sting operation in world history between 2015-2024.

The breakthrough came when Ward received a tip from a trusted source within the global intelligence community. The source directed him to a network of secret vaults located deep within remote regions, protected by some of the world's most elite forces. Ward's source also provided crucial intelligence suggesting that these reserves had been amassed over centuries by secret societies and were intended to fund the deep state's operations. Ward knew that if this gold could be liberated, it would fundamentally shift the balance of power in the global economy.

With this intel in hand, Ward convened a hidden band of experts that included financial insiders to ex-military operatives and blockchain developers. Their task: to find, secure and transfer these hidden reserves into the QFS. It was a high-stakes gamble, with agents going undercover in multiple countries — but Ward and his crew didn't back down. They realized too much was at risk to fail. If they won, the global financial system would change forever.

Months of meticulous planning and execution had led Ward's team to a set of underground vaults in the mountains, but the region was one that few rarely ventured into They discovered reserves that were biblical - gold bars loaded up higher than the eye could see; each holding within it, the potential to rewrite not just global finance as we know today. No longer the reserves of a deep state out to exploit them, these resided in the public domain. Through this Ward knew that he could do for XRP what had eluded Ripple, back it with gold and so finally provide the cryptocurrency world a massive, game-changing coin to save the financial world and offer peace of mind needed during the greatest stock market crash in world history in 2025.

Ward's discovery couldn't have come at a better moment. There was chaos in financial markets around the world like never before witnessed. Fiat currencies were — and still are — hemorrhaging due to their inherent debts, hyperinflations rose in each of the major economies, trust into central banking activity hit an all-time low. The people were awakening and the governments scrambled to ensure their control. Their promise of the central banks and fiat money was no longer believed. They wanted a new way of doing things and XRP backed by gold provided that alternative.

Having secured the reserves, Ward then moved onto phase two of his plan: integrating the gold into QFS and supporting XRP with it. That called for nothing less than the smartest game-theoretical economists and cryptographic minds in both blockchain development and economics. Both were based on the Ripple Protocol Consensus Algorithm and would allow XRP to remain fast, scalable, secure while serving as what was anticipated could be the world's first gold-backed digital currency, XRP+. The team started to work on a concept in which every single piece of XRP can be tied against an amount of gold backed in vaults that are fully audited by a decentralized network validators.

41

The introduction of gold-backed XRP sent shockwaves through the global financial markets. For years, XRP had been touted as the future of digital payments, but now it had become much more. It was no longer just a cryptocurrency — it was the foundation of a new financial order. As word of Ward's discovery spread, demand for XRP skyrocketed. Investors, governments, and even corporations rushed to buy XRP, recognizing that it was now one of the most stable assets in the world. The tokenization of assets, from real estate to commodities, followed suit, as XRP's liquidity and transparency enabled the seamless transfer of value across borders and industries.

One of the immediate effects of Ward's gold-backed XRP was the collapse of fiat currencies. With central banks unable to print unlimited amounts of money and no longer able to manipulate the value of their currencies, the global financial system began to shift towards decentralization. XRP became the de facto global reserve currency, while central banks were left scrambling to maintain relevance. The deep state, which had long profited from the manipulation of fiat currencies, was powerless to stop the rise of XRP.

The QFS, powered by blockchain technology and quantum computing allowed to reach higher statures of transparency in the financial system that has never existed in human recorded history. Corrupt politicians and bankers could not carry out illicit activities in secret anymore. All transactions on The XRP ledger will be visible to the public, providing transparency fully and hopefully making such highlights of financial crimes as well. Some governments that had permanently resorted to secrecy and corruption were laid bare, ultimately losing their legitimacy as a result of the lies spun by those in power.

Over the next few years, a new global financial system emerged that was better adapted to fairness and transparency — more decentralized. XRP gold became the centerpiece of that economy, trading aligned with commerce and investment drove what was now a worldwide GDP. Asset tokenization took off, permitting everyone from the average Joe to institutional investors fractional ownership of luxury real estate or even a Picasso. The unprecedented situation where very few have wealth and the rest go to work for them days were over, a new financial revolution was upon us and we are handing the keys to unlock trillions of dollars on the XRPL, through making the official XRP token as the gas of the entire financial world.

The mere fact that Ward had found the hidden gold reserves, changed history forever. Not only did his actions guarantee the success of the Quantum Financial System, XRP had become the number one valuable digital asset in the world, they also secured a better future for those born into it. Life will never be lived as slaves to an old financial order. Organized financial corruption has been rooted out and the deep state Cabal could no longer control our money or fund their wicked crimes against humanity.

The QFS grew and changed with the rest of the world throughout the 2030s, incorporating modern technologies such as quantum computing solutions. It established XRP as the gold backing of a new global digital economy, one that had proven itself through every wavering storm and outperformed nearly all other assets in its stability and security. However, Ward was not done yet. He was still supervising that the QFS continued to be kept free from those who wanted to use it for their riches, as with any advanced mechanism.

That was just the tip of iceberg when it came to learning where hidden gold deposits lay. Ward was to know that there were still organizations at large in the world who wanted their finger on how money, lending and debt worked globally -and he would be damned if those groups took control. He, along with his allies at the QFS would continue their struggle for financial freedom bolstered by a growing global movement that knew the battle for control of Earth wealth was far from over.

From underground sleuth to one of the most prominent figures and architects in contemporary finance, Ward had a remarkable journey. His relentless pursuit of the truth and a rare combination of experience in part Indiana Jones and part Tesla had made him able to do what many believe is undoable — create a real decentralized gold backed money that would forever change the financial world for generations to come. Ward, through XRP and the QFS had just handed to the world its future out of all that past manipulation and corruption; financial freedom available for every living man and woman on earth with limitless entrepreneurial and charitable opportunities to make the world a better place and glorify God on the road to redemption.

8

Innocent Dreams become Visionary Art and Music

In the early 2020s, the world was in turmoil as it had never been before—economic collapse followed by political upheaval followed by revelations of decades-long secrets. In my art, I tried to distill these massive shifts into their essence in the language of symbolism, prophecy and biting political commentary. It was all buried in my work: each creation with its ulterior motive, the poems and stories bundled away as casual literature — but beneath every line that

invisible fight for mankind's heart. All my original pieces are signed with the letters "B.J.C." which to me, means "Because Jesus Christ" and as a reminder of one of my life's verses: I can do all things through Christ who strengthens me. These events occurred to glorify God, and these strokes of the brush are but His hand at work!

April of 2021 I painted a tribute to General Michael Flynn One of the heroes in America and pivotal figure in this Q movement The painting showed Flynn not as a soldier, but as the truth warrior who helped launch Trump into a covert operation by American soldiers to ferret out foreign corruptors and uphold the Constitution. The picture was, for Flynn honoring and encouraging a man going through unrighteous persecution became symbols forever of his determination to practice freedom and fight for justice. His loyalty to the American people and part of Trump's behind-the-scenes secret plan to take down the deep state became a source of hope for patriots all around. This image cast Flynn as a warrior-superhero, defending the Republic in secret for its own good.

"Checkmate: Trump vs. the World" (March 2021) became one of the most powerful pieces in this collection. This artwork depicted Donald Trump seated confidently at a table, surrounded by world leaders who looked on in shock and guilt as Trump revealed the *COVID-19 Fauci Dossier.* The leaders' complicity in the global mishandling of the pandemic and its far-reaching consequences had been exposed, and Trump was in the position of truth, ready to reveal the deception. Each figure—from **Vladimir Putin** to **Xi Jinping**, **Hillary Clinton**, and **Barack Obama**—symbolized their respective roles in these global crimes, from misinformation campaigns to suppression of crucial evidence about the virus's origins.

Trump's firm grip on the *Fauci Dossier* was symbolic of the awakening happening across the world. The dossier was not just about Fauci's involvement in the pandemic but about the entire network of global elites who had exploited the crisis to consolidate their power. A *Holy Bible* rested beside Trump, representing his reliance on faith and divine justice to lead the way forward, as well as the underlying spiritual battle between good and evil. Inscribed on the table in Chinese was the message: *"Repent and believe in Jesus Christ alone to be saved."* The message extended beyond the political figures, calling for humanity to turn toward faith in a time of moral and societal collapse. Please know that Dr. David Martin deserves to be commemorated and acknowledged in his role of writing the "Fauci Dossier" which provided evidence of documented crimes against humanity. Dr. Martin is an american hero who should be invited into the Trump Administration with Robert F. Kennedy Jr.. Dr. Martin helped to expose the plandemic of COVID-19 and other vaccine patent fraud and crimes against humanity in his free book "Fauci Dossier" published in early 2021 available at DavidMartin.world

OBAMA, DON'T PISS OFF A PRESIDENT
WHO CAN KICK YOUR ASS

This work sits in a lineage of prophesy pieces I've been producing since 2013, each one prefiguring major events within the collapse globally. That year, I created a painting titled "Obama Don't Piss Off A President Who Can Kick You Ass" that showed Barack Obama and Vladamir Putin wrestling to the death before being eradicated by nuclear explosion. The image encapsulates the era's beadle from a geopolitically angle at which point, their moves would foster global corruption and eventually manifest in exploitation of the pandemic. The mushroom cloud symbolized the ever more dangerous crises of our globalized world, in politics but also in many covert wars through manipulation and control.

Fast forward to 2020, and I produced "Trump vs. Biden = Rocky vs. Drago" depicting Donald Trump and Joe Biden in a boxing match. While Biden would eventually win the 2020 election, the artwork was never about a single political moment—it was a prophecy of Trump's ongoing battle against entrenched corruption and ultimately knocking him out of the race in 2024. The boxing ring became a symbol of the larger struggle between Trump and the deep state, with the battle transcending elections and moving into the arena of global power dynamics. The Russian and Ukrainian flag logos were foretelling the corruption to be exposed about the Biden Crime family.

In **2022**, I released *"Cousins at Arms: RFK Jr. and JFK Jr."* which imagined both **RFK Jr.** and **JFK Jr.** standing side by side as political leaders. At the time, the artwork was viewed as speculative, but when **RFK Jr.** announced his candidacy for the 2024 election and aligned himself with Trump's campaign, the painting gained a prophetic significance. The image hinted at the return of **JFK Jr.**, subtly marked by the **Q logos** on their collars—a symbol that tied them to the Q movement and the deeper truths being revealed.

Another of my significant works, *"The Great Reset" (2024)*, depicted the collapse of the old financial system. In this piece, a decapitated bronze bull lay in ruins, representing the fall of **Wall Street** and the traditional banking powers. Rising from the ashes was a futuristic city, built on decentralized principles with **XRP** and the **Quantum Financial System (QFS)** at its core. The imagery foretold the **2025 financial collapse**, which sent ripples across the global economy, forcing a shift toward decentralized currencies and systems, and marking the dawn of a new financial era.

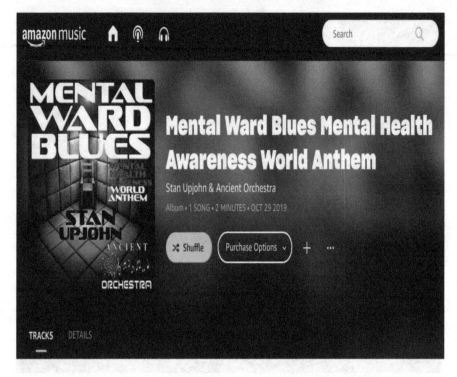

Amid these seismic shifts in politics and finance, I also addressed personal and societal struggles with the release of *"Mental Ward Blues: Mental Health Awareness World Anthem"* on **October 29, 2019**. This song, written during my own experience of unlawful detention in a mental health facility in **2013**, was a response to the trauma of enduring severe medication withdrawal and the broken system that misunderstood those suffering from mental health issues compared to those with traumatic brain injuries or post traumatic stress injury (aka PTSD). The song, sung in a parody style of **Johnny Cash's Folsom Prison Blues** by **Anthony Vincent** of **10 Second Songs**, called for reform and raised awareness of the psychological and systemic issues within the mental health care system. Its release coincided with a growing global recognition of mental health crises, making it an anthem for change in a world struggling with both individual and collective trauma. Seek the Lord Jesus Christ, He renews minds, He restores souls and give us a new heart for Him. His grace is sufficient for thee (all of us).

In the end, this is how all my prophetic pieces of writing come to a close in Revelation 19 showing us Jesus Christ returning for good and as King of KIngs and Lord of Lords. As with the other works noted above, in this painting I wish to visualize a Biblically with scriptural influence for the most accurate descriptions of a final vision and describing the final battle of the bible. As Christ comes riding into this magnificent scene on a white horse, He is followed by the armies of heaven (children of God) to vanquish Satan and all his fallen angels in that final battle for dominion over earth. It is an image of final triumph — Jesus coming with the sword in His mouth (He is the Word of God), and His robe dipped in blood to defeat Satan or that Ancient Serpent who led the world astray; He casts them along their demonic forces into the lake of fire forever.

The last war is not only the end of material evil but also God's merciful will to deliver and keep men from being lost. Indeed the fire that burned and never got extinguished was anciently prepared for the devil and his fallen angels, oh but unless there is a Savior in Jesus Christ, all us sinners would go unto eternity wasted in exactly this same everlasting hell. However, we are given salvation through Jesus Christ and His Good News, where on the cross He declared "It is Finished", which meant the wages of sin, which is death was paid once for all. He rose again 3 days later and was witnessed by hundreds and then 40 days later, He ascended into heaven where He went to prepare a place for us in glory in heaven and His return will be the ultimate closing curtain of humanity and final ending place for Satan and his demons in eternity in a lake of fire.

Combined, these works write a complete story that had already predicted what is now happening the world over. General Flynn military Q operations with Q+ Trump, Checkmate and artwork for a Fauci Dossier distribution campaign for global corruption disclosure, Wall Street's symbolic fall, exposing MK Ultra and mental health reform — The pieces to the Moment of TRUTH In my work in art I have attempted to capture this financial, political and spiritual reset that is taking place in the world around us because this event will be one of if not the pivotal moment for everyone and everything else on planet Earth as we experience now.

The message remains the same through all eternity: God is in control and He prepared good works before mankind to walk faithfully in. For the glory of Jesus, our Lord and Savior. If we seek Him with all our heart, mind and strength, everything else will follow. Never give up, no matter how hard your destiny in life may be. The world really needs you so much right now. Together with love, kindness, prayer and unity in Christ, we will overcome this evil for good.

Remember, Jesus already won the victory, walk in victory and meditate on the last verses in the bible, Revelation 22:18-21, "For I testify to everyone who hears the words of the prophecy of this book: If anyone adds to these things, God will add to him the plagues that are written in this book; and if anyone takes away from the words of the book of this prophecy, God shall take away his part from the Book of Life, from the holy city, and *from* the things which are written in this book. He who testifies to these things says, "Surely I am coming quickly." Amen. Even so, come, Lord Jesus! The grace of our Lord Jesus Christ *be* with you all. Amen.

9

The 2025 Stock Market Crash

In the year of 2025, a worldwide financial disaster triggered by both Tether (USDT) and U.S. dollar (USD) collapsing has devastated all monetary systems available to mankind. A dual beheading of a financial snake atop a falling spiral of global markets whose epicenter became the shuddering site of these economic systems crumbling in a catastrophic collapse. This market turmoil crushed the flagging stock markets. This crash of crashes set off a series of cascading events which stripped away the existing control mechanisms and resulted in what has been predicted to be the most seismic financial collapse since 1929. However, through all this chaos there were two unprecedented emerge from the wreckage to restore law and order in the financial world, XRP & The Quantum Financial System (QFS) as pillars of stability ultimately holding society back towards its center.

Warning Signs: Crash Ahead

Long before the fateful events of 2025, the seeds had been sown for a stock market crash on an epic scale. The global economy had been based on fiat currencies for nearly six decades and U.S dollar was king back then. But the system was already starting to crack as early as 2020, when Covid exposed large fraud in medical and pharmaceutical industry along with weakened global supply chains, medical crimes against humanity and the financial crimes against humanity created indebted solitude with a necessity for infinite QE not only out of central banks but governments. Please know it was the "white hats", the largest secret military sting operation in world history and some of the brightest minds in America who foresaw all of this and even planned disclosure with crafted foresight and deep forethought to cause the least amount of damage to the societal structure.

In the years leading up to 2025, economic experts had warned of the unsustainable nature of fiat currencies, particularly the USD and USDT, which had been propped up by artificial monetary policies and rampant money printing. Tether, the most widely used stablecoin, had long been criticized for its lack of transparency and questionable backing by actual assets. These warning signs were largely ignored by policymakers and financial institutions, who remained entrenched in the belief that the dollar, banks, FDIC and USDT were too big to fail.

However, as inflation spiraled out of control and trust in centralized financial institutions waned, the stage was set for a monumental collapse. In the final days of 2024, the financial markets began to tremble, and by early 2025, the tipping point was reached and the petrified traders sold off everything and dumped much of the stop losses into crypto ETFs that had recently been added to the exchange. This saved 90% of most retirees mutual fund and treasury bond investments and sent Bitcoin, Ethereum and XRP to new all-time highs and created the first institutional bull run that saved the American economy.

The Collapse of the USD and USDT

The U.S. dollar had been dying a slow death — ruined by decades of irresponsible financial policy, insider trading, simmering geopolitical discord and growing economic disparities. With inflation running rampant, the Fed lowered and raised interest rates back and forth to try stimulate the economy — but all that did was make things worse. As a result, global confidence in the dollar plummeted and nations started to unload shares of American firms on the stock market and most foretelling started dumping U.S. Treasury Bonds, weakening it further.

At the same time, Tether was a house of cards waiting to collapse. USDT was the cornerstone stable coins of stable coins and served as a lifeblood for keeping liquidity around in suffocated crypto space. But when investigations of Tether's reserves emerged, the stalls appeared on all fronts and a panic began. In response, traders frantically started selling their USDT which sparked a massive sell-off across the crypto-ecosystem. What had been thought of as a stablecoin and protective hedge to treacherous volatility was now contributing to the financial contagion.

The global markets went into full-on panic, as both the USD and USDT crashed. Stock exchanges the world over stopped trading as indices hit record lows. In the US, in a few days Dow Jones Industrial Average and S&P 500 lost 66% of their value — hundreds of billions of dollars vanished. Goldman Sachs, JPMorgan, TD Bank and Wells Fargo: These financial institutions—once pillars of the global economic system —crumbled in just minutes from an onslaught of panic liquidation orders including their own corporate stock collapsing, almost "end of FightClub" style, falling faster than the World Trade Center under controlled demolition.

XRP and the QFS: Beacons of Stability

As chaos ensued from the ripple effect of financial market and currency collapse, XRP and the Quantum Financial System stood out as rare beacons of stability for individuals, corporations and governments alike. Cross-border payments and liquidity massively expanded with the digital asset and future of finance, XRP. Those that understood the underlying technology -- Ripple's Consensus Ledger, which powers XRP— saw an opportunity to showcase a digital asset class with unheard of speed and security.

While the rest of the planet mourned a world with no fiat currencies, XRP skyrocketed, Ripple became the largest IPO in world history on the XRP Stock Market. XRP, a decentralized digital asset, was not controlled at will by any one organization or government or central banking cartel — in stark contrast to the centralized fiat systems they had seen collapse so publicly. XRP was secure, it was transparent and could be settled in seconds — perfect for a world disintegrating financially. Governments, corporations and even Central Banks started using XRP for settlements outside their imploding legacy financial systems, like Swift payments and American Clearing House (ACH) were replaced overnight.

Central to this revolution was the Quantum Financial System (QFS), a ground-breaking, blockchain-based structure which had pledged to replace all old systems of control with open-source and non-centralized institutions. For years the QFS, managed by financial professionals like Charlie Ward, have been eagerly awaiting this opportunity to deploy. This moment is what the collapse of USD and USDT gave us, following which QFS fired up stabilizing global economy.

The QFS was much more than a new financial system it completely altered the way money and assets were tracked, traded and stored. Once again, the QFS was made fail-safe as it got rid of 3rd Party manipulation and interference by going to a fully decentralized system, the new financial paradigm was revealed after the dust settled, the initial XRP holders were the world's new millionaires and billionaires, founders become trillionaires overnight. The secret sauce of the QFS was that it utilized XRP to give real-time liquidity and speed with which to process transactions.

The Tokenization of Assets

The Quantum Financial System and XRP were part of a wider deployment concerning the tokenization of global assets. Tokenization enabled the representation of both physical and financial assets on the blockchain, thereby enabling them to be easily tradable and interchange, divisible and most importantly liquid. For the first time in history, real estate, commodities, stocks and bonds (including national debts), and even intellectual property could be tokenized on the XRP Ledger for instant settlement with full transparency of exchange.

Ownership, and transfer of assets had been entangled with intermediaries, bureaucracy and lacked transparency for centuries. Such a reality was no longer feasible with the tokenization process where assets would now pass from one hand to another across borders without restrictions and away from intermediaries like banks or governments.

59

For example, a real estate property in London could be tokenized and sold in fractions to investors in Tokyo, New York, and Johannesburg—all in real-time, thanks to the efficiency of the XRP Ledger. This newfound liquidity not only unlocked previously illiquid markets but also democratized access to wealth, allowing individuals to invest in assets that were once the exclusive domain of the ultra-wealthy similar to the Island Project in Hawaii.

A new global currency was needed, as the world tried to cope with the aftermath of US dollar collapse. Enter XRP. Not to mention that XRP can provide a quick and secure way for the settlement of payments, it is indeed seen as being ready on its own integration with QFS over gold-backed System, integrated into unhackable Starlink and SpaceX satellites working seamlessly on the XRPL, XRP is, quite literally, sent to the moon. These countries that appeared to be swapping their dollar dependency began using XRP to make transactions throughout the global economy. Due to XRP being decentralized; no single country or entity could fully control it, therefore serving as a neutral and fair currency for global trade.

XRP was also many times more scalable and liquid, which again makes it a perfect choice for the needs of humanity as exchange. This is important for the rapid settlements of XRP transfers, since QFS provides liquidity system not only to that level at which fiat currency can be cashed and sold or transferred elsewhere—its blockchain transparency guarantees quick verification of the underlying transaction.

This transformation occurred as XRP became the reserve currency, resulting in a transfer of power from financial centers like Wall Street and the City of London to other parts of world. In short, QFS did not allow a monetary system controlled by the so-called elites; it instead puts power in the hands of every participant on earth.

The Aftermath: A New Financial Order

The 2025 stock market crash and dollar collapse changed the world forever. The previous financial systems with centralized control and manipulation had crumbled to be replaced by a transparent, liquid, fair system of our very own. Ripple and QFS became the two pillars of this new financial regime, providing a decentralized and non-manipulable foundation for the world economy.

Through all of the death and suffering that came with this crash, it was also an opportunity to start over. The world had a shot at resorting itself — to build an economic system which would function for all, and not just the few. The tokenization of assets, the launch of XRP as the new reserve currency and deployment of QFS were all signs that ushered in a more decentralized world where power and wealth would be widely shared.

As the dust settled, it became clear that the 2025 stock market crash was not just a financial event—it was a turning point in human history. The collapse of the USD and USDT had exposed the flaws in the old system, and in its place, a new system had risen, built on blockchain technology, transparency, and decentralization.

XRP and the QFS were not just tools for financial transactions— they were the foundation of a new world system of justice, one where financial freedom and equality were finally within reach for all. The future was uncertain, but one thing was clear: the old ways of doing business were gone, and a new era of decentralized finance had dawned.

XRP and the DTCC – Revolutionizing Global Transactions

This is a historic game-changer, as XRP is named the official payment flow for Depository Trust & Clearing Corporation (DTCC) and global finance. Considering that the DTCC handles $1.6 quadrillion in trades every year, the availability of XRP into this ecosystem is a major milestone for blockchain tech and decentralized finance as well. Though the implications are wide, such a system can lead to increased transparency and superior efficiency in clearing and settlement processes.

As the spine of U.S. financial markets, DTCC has been looking at digital transformation for quite some time through projects such as Project Ion to support accelerated settlement using distributed ledger technology (DLT). Utilizing XRP as its settlement asset, DTCC is entering a new era of frictionless instant and secure transactions that will revolutionize the way in which global money moves. This is the digital cheerio, the digitization of cash and securities with XRP as a bridge asset for institutional value transfer.

The Integration: XRP as the Backbone of Global Settlement

DTCC's use of XRP to settle is an important diversion from legacy systems which are plagued by costly and antiquated inefficiencies, like settlement delays (currently T+2) or exorbitant liquidity capital requirements. These transactions can almost settle in real time and without the need of an intermediary due to XRP blockchain technology with real time settlement, atomic transfers.

For the $1.6 quadrillion annual transactions that flow through DTCC, XRP demand is about to go ballistic as all of those proceed through the XRPL! This huge amount of transactions are going to take place in just nanoseconds and also will eliminate all the transaction frictions that we have been seeing over the years in any financial sector. This is where the occasion dictates the ground for a significant part of XRP burn. Each and every transaction that goes through the platform will consume some XRP tokens, burning these at a slow pace to slowly decrease the supply of XRP on average over time while making it even scarcer than before.

Price Implications: Skyrocketing XRP

With XRP now underpinning the **world's largest financial clearinghouse**, its value is set to rise exponentially. The combination of high transaction volume, the **burn mechanism**, and **wallet lockups** will drastically reduce the circulating supply of XRP, pushing its price higher as demand increases. The **finite supply of 100 billion XRP tokens** means that as more institutions adopt XRP, and as more transactions flow through the system, the upward pressure on its price will be immense.

The DTCC's shift to XRP-based settlements also introduces **wallet lockups**, where significant portions of XRP are held in reserve to ensure liquidity across the financial system. These lockups will take millions, if not billions, of XRP out of circulation, reducing the available supply even further.

A Financial Revolution: Transparency, Efficiency, and Trust

Overall, XRP's implementation in the DTCC is more than a technological update – rather, it is the first step toward a new era of finances. Every transaction will be transparent thanks to the blockchain, eliminating the opacity which was a fertile ground for financial crimes and inefficiencies. In addition, the XRP Ledger will enable a secure and unalterable record of each transaction, lowering the risk of fraud and increasing the level of trust in the world's financial system. The speed and low cost of each transaction on the XRPL, which will save the financial sector billions of dollars. The DTCC's choice to utilize XRP in its $1.6 quadrillion transactions per year demonstrates the blockchain technology's efficiency and scalability. The global financial markets will no longer operate on outdated and slow infrastructure and mechanisms, but instead, they will run based on a futuristic and innovative platform capable of completely reforming the way money flows.

The Future of Global Finance

DTCC adopting XRP is a historical moment in finance. With blockchain set to power the world largest finance transaction clearinghouse, XRP is poised become more than just a link in the financial chain, it's foundation the XRPL is the backbone of a whole new financial system. Through its shareholders and buyback incentives Ripple, after the IPO will propel XRP to never-before-seen price ratios and establish a basis for an era when blockchain technology is integral part of every aspect in global finance.

With XRP token burns with each transaction and billions locked-up in reserves, its scarcity will become a marketing point that goes up with it's value. This is the financial revolution, and XRP sits right at it's epicenter full of promises that we should experience an entirely transparent, lightning fast, economically responsible and secure global economy.

Part III

The New Economic Paradigm

10

Military Tribunals and Nesara-Gesara

The idea behind Nesara (National Economic Security and Reformation Act) along with its global version, Gesara (Global Economic Security and Reformation Act) has always been a source of fascination in the world by financial conspiracy theorists. But, with its calls for things like a debt jubilee and the gold-backed currency system that existed before August 15th of 1971, if this movement ends up successfully carrying through on at least some of these proposals it will be proposing one radical overhaul to global economics. The process of ending the fiat currency, through which Nesara and Gesara reforms are implemented with XRP at the center.

Introduction to Nesara-Gesara

Nesara and Gesara were designed to address the systemic financial corruption entrenched within global banking institutions. At its core, these reforms aim to redistribute wealth more equitably and create financial systems built on transparency, accountability, and sustainability. By eliminating corrupt financial practices like fractional reserve banking and introducing debt forgiveness, Nesara-Gesara seeks to restore balance to the global economy.

When the U.S. dollar collapsed in 2025, it triggered the worldwide implementation of Nesara-Gesara. Governments and central banks, which had long manipulated the global economy for their own interests, were rendered powerless. In their place, a new system of governance, based on blockchain transparency, emerged. XRP, with its decentralized nature and speed of transaction, became the foundation for this financial reset.

Military Tribunals: A Reckoning for Financial Crimes

Concurrent with the economic reset, worldwide tribunals took place and were live streamed on X.com (formerly Twitter) and Rumble.com and archived for the world to see, as a reminder of what never should happen in history again — from dark to light. The purpose of these tribunals was to name and prosecute the corrupt global elite bankers who were responsible for causing the financial collapse. In a series of high-profile arrests, central bankers, corporate executives and politicians were charged for decades-long fraud cabals connected to insider trading scams through the laundering of trillions in stolen money which had been stolen away from global populations.

To allow the alleged perpetrators to be brought before courts where defending themselves was possible, two tribunals against such individuals were implemented as military tribunal that normally only applies when martial law is in effect. There was simply not an end to the level of accountability needed and — even more fundamentally — systems were being investigated, reworked to uproot a culture desiring to expose and oust this kind of flagrant corruption. The trials were shown on public television, in keeping with the spirit of transparency under way in the new economic system. To many, it was a much-needed coming-to-Jesus moment in the reckoning of Justice and how trust would be restored in a new financial world order.

It was not just financial crimes that these tribunals targeted. They also exposed deep state actors using their power to control governments and economies, for personal profit. As the trials went on, it came out in evidence that a concerted effort by global elite to bring down other economical systems like XRP and Quantum Financial System which was being aimed as an alternative to this imploding fiat Central Bank global dominance.

XRP and the Tokenization of Wealth

Nesara and Gesara through, XRP was the centerpiece of a new financial system The crux of this evolution lay in the concept called tokenization. In the old financial world, wealth was held in holding physical assets – like gold or real estate — but most of us were excluded from these asset types if we did not have enough capital to participate. Tokenization of real world and virtual assets by XRP Ledger smart contracts, for the people— democratized ownership of money only a few years ago, making each type as accessible as owning very small individual pieces of these assets.

For instance, gold reserves — having been balled-up in central banks and corrupt financial elite for millennia were henceforth isolated as cryptographic tokens with distribution on the XRP ledger through the efforts of Charlie Ward. This was how it worked with real estate, art and other collectibles, intellectual property including patents, even stocks. This new financial ecosystem allowed users to invest in and trade a variety of assets, entirely secured on an open and transparent blockchain.

Tokenization also introduced unprecedented liquidity to the market. Traditional financial systems often struggled with the transfer of physical assets, but tokenized assets could be traded instantly. This increased liquidity not only stabilized the economy during the post-crash period but also encouraged further investment and innovation.

Debt Forgiveness and Financial Liberation

One of the most immediate impacts of the Nesara and Gesara reforms were the widespread implementation of debt forgiveness. Under the old system, debt was a tool used by financial institutions to control populations and maintain power. Loans, mortgages, credit cards, and student debts had burdened millions, making true financial freedom almost impossible.

With the collapse of fiat currencies and the implementation of a gold-backed system powered by XRP, debt was restructured and, in many cases, forgiven entirely. This was not just a symbolic gesture—it was a tangible way of redistributing wealth and providing individuals with a fresh start. The debt forgiveness program also included the dismantling of predatory lending practices, such as adjustable variable rate loans, the elimination and reparations of interest on loans, further reducing the financial burden on everyday citizens.

As debt disappeared, so too did the societal structures that had kept populations in a cycle of poverty. The post-debt world opened new opportunities for entrepreneurship, homeownership and financial independence. For the first time, individuals had the freedom to pursue their passions and build wealth without the constraints of a corrupt financial system.

Transparency in Global Systems

The most considerable success of the QFS Powered by XRP was its ability to bring clarity to world's financial systems. In the traditional world, we could say that all financial transactions were veiled because central banks do what they want and no one knows about it. Corruption, money laundering and insider trading were all the time present – but hidden behind a black box for tax payers knowing nothing of what actually took place.

The QFS changed that. Entirely transparent and immortalized through blockchain technology, every QFS transaction was recorded by satellites. This meant that no transaction could be altered or concealed, and all transactions were visible to everyone on the network in real-time. This level of transparency was a significant blow to all financial institutions and governments.

Corrupt practices like tax evasion and money laundering were nearly impossible in the new system. Every financial transaction was traceable, and any attempt to manipulate the system was immediately flagged and addressed. Governments, too, were held accountable for their spending, as citizens could now track how their tax dollars were being used.

This transparency extended beyond financial transactions. Under the Nesara and Gesara reforms, governance structures were reimagined to ensure that public officials were also held accountable. Blockchain technology was used to record and verify political decisions, creating a system where corruption could not thrive.

Wealth Redistribution and Global Equality

The old financial systems imploded and the wealth went belly up. Wealth had been overly concentrated for centuries into the hands of a handful and was still making life difficult for most people around the world. Nesara and Gesara somewhat remedy this problem by an fair redistribution of wealth, yet also encourage capitalism to continue for the entrepreneurial creators on earth. The significance XRP played in facilitating this wealth transfer cannot be undervalued. These firsts included asset-tokenization and the origin of debt forgiveness, which meant that anyone could access wealth once hoarded by an aristocracy. Not in the sense of stealing from people that are struggling and giving to them, nor creating equality by making everyone poor, but instead as a way for "all boats to rise together with the tide". Every human on earth was offered the exact same financial services, and Outliers were no longer stranded outside of the dream as it is no more — all humans could financially prosper in harmony if they felt so inclined to do.

This redistribution of wealth had a profound impact on global society. Poverty rates plummeted as individuals gained access to financial resources that had previously been out of reach. Education, healthcare, and housing were no longer luxuries, but basic human rights that could be afforded by all. The ripple effects of this wealth redistribution were felt across every sector of society, as new opportunities for growth and innovation emerged.

The Role of the QFS in Stabilizing the Global Economy

As the Nesara and Gesara reforms took hold, the global economy began to stabilize. The Quantum Financial System, backed by XRP and gold reserves, provided the foundation for a new era of financial stability. Unlike the old system, which was prone to crashes and manipulation, the QFS was designed to be resilient and transparent.

The QFS's blockchain technology allowed for real-time settlement of transactions, reducing the risk of fraud and ensuring that all financial dealings were secure. This created a sense of trust in the new system that had been absent from the old one. Investors, who had once been wary of the volatility of the stock market, began to reinvest in the global economy, confident in the stability of the QFS.

Moreover, the QFS eliminated the need for intermediaries like banks and brokers. Individuals and businesses could now conduct transactions directly, without the need for third-party approval or unnecessary wealth management fees of the past. This not only reduced transaction costs but also increased efficiency, allowing the global economy to recover more quickly from the 2025 crash.

The Global Impact of Nesara and Gesara Reforms

Nesara and Gesara were not just a U.S. plan it was global. This was replicated in countries around the world as well, and many realized that the outdated fiat currency system with central banks had finally run its course. The world was transitioning to a comprehensive, more transparent financial system with the help of QFS and XRP in collaboration between many Nations.

The new economic paradigm particularly benefited developing nations. For hundreds of years, their countries had been looted and plundered by the global economic elite for as long as they can remember in cycles of indebtedness without end. All they had to do was "flick the switch": Nesara-Gesara provided them a safe landing. Tokenized asset and debt forgiveness opened up the opportunity for these nations to rebuild their economies, provide opportunities for growth and prosperity to its citizens.

The global adoption of Nesara-Gesara also led to a shift in geopolitical power. The old world order, dominated by a few powerful nations and financial institutions, was replaced by a more balanced and inclusive system. Power was no longer concentrated in the hands of a few elites but distributed across a global network of individuals and communities.

The Nesara-Gesara reforms, powered by XRP and the Quantum Financial System, ushered in a new era of financial freedom and transparency. The collapse of the old financial systems, while painful, provided an opportunity for the world to rebuild on a foundation of fairness and accountability. With the tokenization of assets, debt forgiveness, and the redistribution of wealth, individuals were empowered to take control of their financial futures.

The military tribunals and the exposure of financial crimes ensured that those who had exploited the old system were held accountable. As the world moved forward, the lessons of the past were not forgotten, and the new financial paradigm was built to ensure that such corruption could be exploited and would not have the opportunity to arise again. As the 2025 stock market crash gave way to the implementation of the Quantum Financial System and Nesara-Gesara reforms, the world entered a new era of financial transparency, fairness, and stability.

Nesara-Gesara, once considered a radical and fringe idea, became the backbone of the global economy, guided by XRP and blockchain technology. The tokenization of wealth, coupled with debt forgiveness and wealth redistribution, created a more equitable and inclusive global financial system. With the elimination of corrupt practices, the world moved towards an age of peace and prosperity, where financial transparency and accountability were paramount.

The old world of fiat currencies and centralized banking was gone, replaced by a decentralized and transparent system that empowered individuals and restored trust in global institutions. Nesara-Gesara, with its commitment to fairness and justice, became the blueprint for a better future, and XRP, with its role in the Quantum Financial System, led the way towards a new era of financial freedom.

11

Starlink and Secure Global Communication

Integrating Elon Musk's Starlink satellite constellation with the Quantum Financial System (QFS) marks a new frontier in secure, global communication. Starlink's revolutionary satellite network, originally developed to provide high-speed broadband access, especially in remote areas, has rapidly evolved into a key component of global infrastructure, playing a critical role in the financial and geopolitical reshaping of the world.

The integration of Starlink with the QFS was no accident. It represented a deliberate and strategic move to ensure that the global shift toward a decentralized and transparent financial system would not be undermined by the very forces seeking to control communication channels. By providing secure, encrypted, and unhackable communication pathways, Starlink has effectively safeguarded the flow of financial data and ensured that deep state actors could no longer manipulate global information or block the transmission of sensitive financial data.

The Rise of Starlink: A Revolutionary Communication System

The conception of Starlink by Elon Musk's SpaceX began as an ambitious project to create a low-Earth-orbit (LEO) satellite network capable of providing fast and reliable internet to every corner of the world. As it grew, the system became more than just a tool for internet provision. With thousands of satellites orbiting the Earth, Starlink offered unprecedented global coverage, making it the ideal candidate to merge with the QFS.

What makes Starlink truly exceptional is its Ku-Band downlink technology, which ensures low-latency communication. This technology is at the heart of its ability to revolutionize global positioning, navigation, and timing (PNT), as outlined in a detailed technical document titled *Signal Structure of the Starlink Ku-Band Downlink*. According to this report, the Starlink network uses highly advanced frequency division multiplexing, allowing secure data transmission with extremely low susceptibility to jamming, interference, or hacking. It's everything the QFS needs.

Merging Starlink and QFS: Securing Global Financial Transactions

With the world transitioning to a Quantum Financial System, preventing interference with this new financial infrastructure became paramount. Traditional, centralized systems of control were simply no match for the decentralized constitution and operation of a QFS. But if decentralization was the goal, decentralized solutions would have some forces to reckon with — in this case fraud and solving how a single global ledger could be trusted by everyone for all their asset transfers and many other financial transactions with full transparency.

This is where Starlink's uniqueness shone. Starlink's quality of data transmission with exact timing accuracy has proved extremely useful to split-second trading financial systems high-frequency and cross-border payments. The network's low-earth orbit (LEO) satellites move continuously in space, providing more power and bandwidth than traditional satellite systems so that financial data can be moved securely worldwide.

Furthermore, because Starlink is able to reduce any single point of failure potential that could allow the circulation of financial data to be interrupted. Data has to pass through centralized servers in a traditional communication system which provides for easier access — or hacking. Meanwhile, among the benefits of Starlink global coverage is that it allows for instant takeover by another satellite in case one gets compromised or fails to achieve service continuity.

Combatting Deep State Interference

A critical aspect of Starlink's integration with the QFS was its role in preventing deep state actors from intercepting or manipulating financial data. In the early days of the QFS transition, there were numerous attempts by those clinging to the old fiat systems to undermine the new order. These groups, often referred to as the "cabal," relied on their control of global communication networks to maintain their grip on power.

Starlink's decentralized structure makes it impossible for these actors to control the flow of information. By removing centralized servers and routing financial data through thousands of constantly moving satellites, it is impossible for any single entity to interfere. Moreover, Starlink uses highly encrypted communication channels, ensuring that even if a signal were intercepted, it would be indecipherable without the correct decryption keys, which are protected by quantum encryption methods embedded in the QFS.

This led to a dramatic reduction in financial crimes such as wire fraud, money laundering, and market manipulation, which had plagued the previous centralized systems. Now, all financial transactions were transparent, traceable, and protected by both quantum technology and the global Starlink network.

Securing Communication Beyond Finance: Starlink's Expanded Role

While the integration of Starlink and QFS revolutionized global finance, its implications extend far beyond that. Starlink has become a critical tool in securing communications in other sectors as well, from government to military to voting and even to private enterprise.

One of the most significant aspects of Starlink is its role in securing government communications. In the past, government agencies relied on centralized communication networks that were vulnerable to cyberattacks, surveillance, and sabotage. With Starlink, all government communications can be encrypted and transmitted through the satellite network, ensuring that sensitive information remains secure from adversaries and bad actors. Additionally, Starlink's global reach ensures that even remote government outposts or mobile military units can stay connected.

The military was one of the first to realize the strategic potential of Starlink. In military operations, communication is critical, and the ability to transmit data securely, without fear of interception, can mean the difference between victory and defeat. Starlink has revolutionized military communication by providing secure, real-time data transmission in even the most remote and hostile environments. Whether coordinating airstrikes, sharing intelligence, or communicating with troops on the ground, Starlink ensures that military leaders have the information they need, when they need it.

Additionally, during natural and man-made disasters traditional forms of communication can fail as the network may be destroyed or not capable to carry all necessary traffic. Given Starlink uses a satellite-based infrastructure, it is immune to these disruptions. When the financial crisis hit in 2025, and traditional communication networks collapsed as a result of it; Starlink was instrumental to return global communication. Starlink became the backbone of global communication infrastructure to provide satellite connectivity throughput and capacity that can deploy at a speed which had never been seen before.

Elon Musk's Starlink and QFS integration heralds in a new era of secure, transparent and decentralized global finance. And using the power of thousands of low-Earth orbit satellites, more efficient and less expensive cheaper than satellites kept aloft by NASA, Starlink not only monitors it all, but its network ensures that transactions are also faster and impervious to potential manipulations from those entrenched in traditional legacy interests.

The marriage of quantum technology and blockchain with a satellite-based communication network is the culmination of years of innovation, ushering in a future where the flow of information—and wealth—is distributed fairly and securely. The world has changed irrevocably, and as Starlink's network continues to expand, it will become ever more integral to the new global economic order, ensuring that the corrupt systems of the past will never return. The future of finance, communication, and global governance now rests in the stars.

12

The Quantum Looking Glass, Remote Viewing and Future Projections

I n the unfolding saga of the Quantum Financial Reset, one of the most fascinating and controversial developments is the emergence of technology and practices that allow a select group of individuals to peer into possible future outcomes. Among these, two primary technologies stand out: the Quantum Looking Glass and Remote Viewing. These tools have not only provided insights into the workings of the deep state but have also given key figures like President Donald Trump and John F. Kennedy Jr. the upper hand in thwarting assassination attempts, guiding the Quantum Financial System (QFS), and maintaining XRP's dominance as the foundation of the new financial order.

The Quantum Looking Glass

The concept of the Quantum Looking Glass stretches the boundaries of modern technology. Originally developed as a military tool for strategic advantage, it's been rumored to allow the viewing of probable future timelines. The technology operates on principles of quantum computing and probability projection, leveraging quantum entanglement and metasurfaces to peer into various potential futures. While many regard it as science fiction, those close to the QFS and XRP's rise believe that it played an integral role in orchestrating the collapse of the old fiat-based financial systems and ensuring the success of the new decentralized order.

The Quantum Looking Glass works by visualizing different outcomes based on current decisions and geopolitical events. It's similar to a highly advanced predictive algorithm that maps out a web of possibilities, constantly recalculating as new data comes in. But unlike traditional predictive technologies, the Looking Glass can reveal multiple potential timelines, providing its operators the chance to choose paths that align with their goals. This allowed President Trump and his inner circle to anticipate deep-state actions well in advance, stay ahead of geopolitical manipulation, and maintain XRP's integrity amidst a world of chaos.

In fact, during some of the most pivotal moments in recent history, The Looking Glass was a key player. In the run-up to the collapse of USD (2025), it showed Trump, JFK Jr., and their cadre military advisors exactly how global finance would melt down when QFS went online. They have now chosen the right timeline to stop any more attacks on their presidents, securing XRP and making sure a new economy asset backed Gold securely on the XRPL replaces the US fiat dollar.

Remote Viewing and Intelligence Gathering

One of the powerful tools that has appeared in this war against the deep state is remote viewing, which gained public notoriety in use with CIA research program through American Partnership government projects such like Project Stargate during 1970s and 1980. What originated as the CIA investigating remote viewing for intelligence gathering purposes of foreign operatives has now been expanded by those in QFS to develop and fine-tune to see even further forward. When combined with Quantum Looking Glass, remote viewing allows us to access real-time intelligence on events and locations that we cannot observe physically or currently within this timeline.

Remote viewers—that is, individuals "trained" to project their consciousness across space and time —can potentially access highly detailed information about some remote location or hidden agendas. These are all key in their ability to expose deep-state plots such as medical crimes against humanity with the engineered bioweapon of COVID-19, or multiple assassination attempts upon Trump and JFK Jr. — and to avoid sabotage against the Starlink secured QFS. In the military itself through Space Force, NASA and SpaceX,, subjects of remote viewing also include financial transactions on the blockchain and hidden assets that finance dark money. **We have everything & justice is in the air!**

The **CIA's declassified "Remote Viewing Training Procedures"** shows how these operatives learned to develop their psychic faculties to aid in uncovering plots against the emerging global order. Some reports even suggest that certain high-level military personnel were able to use remote viewing to monitor deep-state actors in real-time, exposing secret communications and financial ties that connected the old elites to illicit activities. This ability to see beyond what was physically observable gave the QFS team an edge, preventing attacks on XRP's infrastructure and guaranteeing the safety of the leaders guiding the new financial system.

JFK Jr.'s Return and the Use of Looking Glass Technology

One of the most dramatic and controversial aspects of the Quantum Looking Glass saga is the return of John F. Kennedy Jr., a figure long thought to have died in a plane crash in 1999. Those close to the Q movement and its offshoots have long speculated that JFK Jr. faked his death, using Looking Glass technology to foresee his assassination and evade it. According to this theory, JFK Jr. stepped out of the public eye and spent decades working with a covert group of military intelligence officials, planning his return at the right moment.

With his alliance with Donald Trump, JFK Jr. became a key figure in orchestrating the financial reset and dismantling the deep-state apparatus. His understanding of time travel and future projection allowed him to stay one step ahead of those who sought to prevent the new world system of justice from taking shape. As the Looking Glass revealed multiple timelines, JFK Jr. and Trump, were able to navigate through them, selecting those that would lead to the collapse of the fiat system, the rise of XRP, and the global adoption of the Quantum Financial System.

The Quantum Financial Reset

The Quantum Financial Reset, made possible by the QFS and XRP, would not have succeeded without the foresight provided by these advanced technologies. By predicting financial crashes and deep-state maneuvers, Trump and JFK Jr. were able to take proactive measures to protect the new decentralized financial order. The deep state, aware that their plans were being thwarted at every turn, made numerous attempts to disrupt the reset through political interference, financial market manipulation, and even assassination attempts. Each time, these efforts were thwarted through a combination of quantum foresight and remote viewing, with the operators behind these technologies consistently staying ahead of the game.

The 2025 Stock Market Crash

In 2025, when the USD finally collapsed under the weight of corruption, it marked the beginning of the global financial crash that many had feared. Wall Street, the symbol of financial corruption and manipulation, was reduced to rubble, both metaphorically and physically. The crash was not just a result of market forces but of strategic moves orchestrated through quantum foresight, ensuring that the crash served as a cleansing event rather than a destructive one.

Both crypto ETFs and the blockchain ledger, particularly XRP, played a crucial role in this transition. With its transparency and immutability, XRP's blockchain ledger exposed the deep-state actors and corrupt financial institutions that had manipulated markets for decades. Insider trading, price-fixing, and market manipulation were laid bare, and the evidence was irrefutable. The ledger also revealed financial transactions tied to assassination attempts on Trump and JFK Jr., implicating some of the world's largest financial institutions in the plots.

The Dow Jones Collapse and the New Financial Order

The collapse of the Dow Jones signaled end times; the shattered bronze head that had been torn from New York's Wall Street symbolized the shattering of the old financial guard. A new city of glass and gold stood in its place, a long visual corridor for the decentralized hubs of the QFS with all transactions visible for the world to witness in real time. The new financial order was powered by XRP, gold backed and quantum secured. It was not just reset, it was a revolution and bring about financial equality globally.

First of all, when the Dow Jones crumbled, it was intentional — Looking Glass operators selected a timeline that would result in not much societal damage while providing optimum opportunities to reconstruct. The blockchain and quantum-based new financial order had been designed to eliminate the corruption, manipulation that existed in their old system. With all assets tokenized on the blockchain, gold-backed XRP is a keystone currency in this brave new world economy — offering full liquidity and transparency to its holders while maintaining fairness across board.

Securing the Future: The Role of Blockchain and Quantum Technology

As the Quantum Financial System continued to develop, blockchain technology and quantum computing became even more integrated. With quantum encryption securing all transactions and communications, deep-state actors found it impossible to manipulate the system. XRP's ledger provided a permanent and unalterable record of all financial transactions, exposing any attempt at fraud or corruption. The transparency of the system ensured that power was distributed among the people, and no longer concentrated in the hands of a few elites.

Quantum computing, particularly the developments made by institutions like **Sandia Laboratories**, played a critical role in processing the massive amounts of data required to keep the QFS running smoothly. These computers, capable of processing information at speeds unimaginable with traditional technology, ensured that the QFS could handle the tokenization of all global assets, from real estate to human capital.

The Ripple Effect of Quantum Technology

The impact of quantum technology extended well beyond the financial world. In answer to their prayers and protection from God, along with special tools such as Looking Glass and remote viewing the timing of which were flawless allowing for global leaders to "flip the switch" enabling XRP and QFS to stay on top in control over the future of financial security and freedom. Yet their impact were woven into every sector of humanity — governance, communication; all elements to ensure the future roamed free under transparency and fairness.

The Quantum Financial Reset was playing out in real time for the whole world to witness. Put another way: What was once sci-fi has indeed become reality, and quantum technology plus blockchain are quite literally changing the very fabric of society. The old paradigms, held together by corruption and avarice dissolved under the irresistible power of transparency and authenticity.

The Quantum Looking Glass, the device that showed Trump, JFK Jr. and military leaders around the world the future had been written, but it was not set: It had been deliberated one decision at the time with our God given free will, seeking to do His will, using the most powerful weapon ever made by humanity — to see beyond now and into what could be.

13

Tokenization of Human Capital

B lockchain technology has taken many fields by storm, allowing for more transparent and decentralized systems all over the world. Leading this revolution is the XRP Ledger (XRPL), which has long been hailed for its speed, scalability and liquidity. As this evolution took place, one of the most revolutionary features it brought in was tokenizing human capital. With the XRP Ledger, tokenization might be developed for human labor and intellectual property — leading to a genuinely digital labor force.

The Concept of Tokenization of Human Capital

At its core, tokenization is the conversion of rights to an asset into a digital token on a blockchain. This has been successfully done with physical assets —think real estate, commodities— but tokenizing human capital is a new frontier. It allows people to tokenize their skills, time and ideas so that they can be traded globally on a decentralized marketplace without the need for intermediaries.

Updated in this way, a person's expertise and labor or intellectual property are expressed as tokens secured with the blockchain. This enables people to maintain more free control of their labor, and creates a globally competitive decentralized market for all human capital.

Tokenizing Intellectual Property and Skills

Think of a freelance software developer in India, marketing consultant in Brazil or writer from the US all who can tokenize their skills and put them on blockchain. By giving their labor and skillsets a physical representation in the form of tokens, workers can then exchange these tokens on an open venue or marketplace which effectively transforms human capital into a liquid trading instrument. The latter would translate to full regulatory freedom for the user and could geographically be offered on a global level. Blockchain also acts as a transparent and immutable ledger which brings more trust on both sides of the transaction —workers can have greater confidence in their accrued wages will be redeemed into any currency worldwide and could even increase in value if held in an interest yielding account staking XRP for RLUSD, whilst employers benefit from much improved efficiency as well.

This vision fits very neatly with the future possibilities Ripple highlight in their ecosystem. Given the high liquidity and speed that they offer, the XRP Ledger represents one of best platform for handling these tokenized assets.

The Global Decentralized Workforce

With the tokenization of human capital coupled with self-banking, we move closer to a future where the global workforce is entirely decentralized. The traditional model of labor markets, where individuals are bound to geographic limitations or middlemen such as recruitment agencies, becomes obsolete. Blockchain technology enables individuals to list their skills on decentralized marketplaces, where employers from anywhere in the world can access their tokens and engage with their services.

A critical component of this system is the decentralization of payments. The XRP Ledger provides an infrastructure where payments for services can be conducted in a seamless, secure, and transparent manner. There is no need for traditional banking intermediaries, which not only speeds up transactions but also lowers costs for all parties involved. Cross-border payments, once complicated and expensive, become instant and cost-effective through the use of XRP.

The Benefits of Tokenizing Human Capital

1. **Empowerment and Ownership** Tokenization provides individuals with full ownership over their skills and intellectual property, transforming the traditional labor dynamic. No longer bound by the constraints of employers or intermediaries who typically control the value of their labor, workers now have direct access to the global marketplace. This open market offers more competitive pricing, driven by transparency and the ability for businesses to connect with talent directly, empowering individuals to take control of their professional worth.

2. **Enhanced Liquidity** Tokenizing labor and intellectual property introduces a new level of liquidity to the job market. Through tokenization, individuals can "sell" portions of their time or skill tokens, broadening their reach and diversifying their income sources. Instead of relying solely on one employer or contract, workers can distribute their expertise across multiple buyers, providing more financial security and flexibility in a decentralized workforce.

3. **Transparency and Security** Blockchain technology ensures that all transactions are both transparent and secure, fostering trust between employers and employees. With every interaction recorded on the blockchain, both parties can verify the authenticity, quality, and completion of work. Smart contracts add another layer of security, automating payments based on pre-agreed terms and minimizing the risk of disputes over deliverables or compensation.

4. **Reduced Fees and Increased Earnings** Traditional freelancing platforms often charge significant fees to connect workers with employers. By operating on decentralized platforms like the XRP Ledger, interactions between workers and companies become more direct, eliminating intermediaries and reducing transaction costs. As a result, individuals can retain more of their earnings, while businesses benefit from lower costs when accessing global talent.

5. **Decentralized Intellectual Property Markets** For creatives, tokenization ensures that they maintain the rights to their intellectual property. A musician, for example, can tokenize a song and sell a portion of future earnings to investors or fans, creating a democratized investment model. This allows supporters to share in the success of creative works, providing both financial backing for artists and potential profits for those who believe in their work. Tokenization thus opens new opportunities for creators to monetize their talents while retaining control over their artistic contributions.

Tokenization and the Future of Education

This is not just about tokenizing our skills and labor but it goes on to change the very construct of how we perceive education. With more decentralized education on the horizon, blockchain technology provides us with a method for tokenizing degrees, certifications and skills. Gives the students verifiable credentials as tokens on blockchain so they can take them with themselves and share it to potential employers all across the globe.

For instance, such a token could be given to a student who successfully completes a coding bootcamp. It is a blockchain-backed token, so employers can verify it easily without relying on any central institution or stored records.

This new model of credentialing offers a way to ensure that skills are easily verified, portable, and resistant to fraud. Blockchain's immutable ledger ensures that once a token is created, it cannot be altered, giving employers confidence in the credentials they are reviewing.

Challenges to Tokenizing Human Capital

As with any innovative technology, the tokenization of human capital presents several challenges. One of the primary issues is the legal and regulatory framework. Many countries still operate within traditional employment laws that don't yet accommodate tokenized labor markets. Questions around taxation, labor rights, and contractual obligations will need to be addressed.

Furthermore, there is the challenge of adoption. While blockchain technology has gained significant traction in the financial sector, its application in labor markets is still nascent. Widespread adoption will require education, regulatory frameworks, and technological infrastructure that can support this new model of employment.

The tokenization of human capital is one of the most fascinating developments to emerge from the blockchain community. This truly has the potential to democratize the workforce on a global scale, giving workers more power over their labor, IPs, and value creation. The XRP Ledger, with its speed and liquidity, is critical for making this happen. As we move towards a more decentralized future, tokenized human capital would give workers the freedom and ability to create value, dismantle clear employment relationships, and create a more true global economy. The blockchain digital revolution in the future of work is coming, and the future of work is now.

14

XRP's Interplanetary Trade and Elon Musk's Occupy Mars Campaign

With hyper-innovations in space exploration and financial technology, humanity is looking forward past Earth to the colonization of other planets. At the center of this story is Elon Musk, SpaceX's visionary founder who has become a global media sensation with his grand "Occupy Mars" banner. The latter takes us to the title of this article — as Musk inches ever closer in his quest for Martian self-sufficiency, a global decentralized currency is also an increasingly necessary premise. For the first time an open digital asset ledger is providing a way to unite world markets in one grand market and giving XRP its place as Earth's key currency for interplanetary trade, made in the image of God on this planet and still searching and dreaming amongst the stars, where our heart lies in the heavens above.

The Vision of Interplanetary Colonization

SpaceX has been driven from the beginning by Elon Musk's vision for humanity to become a multiplanetary species. Musk likes to call Mars "a backup drive for civilization": a hedge against existential threats — say, nuclear war or environmental collapse — that could make the earth uninhabitable. This master plan entails sending the first settlers to Mars on spacecrafts capable of seating more than one hundred people. The end target is a city of one million people on the Red Planet, which Musk expects will take anywhere from forty to over one hundred years to achieve. This timeline nicely coincides with the development of space travel and finance technologies.

An important part of the equation for colonizing Mars is setting up an interplanetary financial system that can function safely and securely. This is where the lightning-fast, ultra-efficient global transactions of XRP step in as an obvious choice for a variety interplanetary financial ecosystem. Since XRP is not a traditional currency, but traded on the blockchain its high-speed and cross border characteristics via SpaceX and Starlink satellites, it makes XRP an ideal candidate for interplanetary trade.

The Collapse of Earth's Financial Systems

Back on Earth, the old financial systems were beginning to crumble under the weight of corruption, debt, and inefficiency. The USD, once the world's reserve currency, saw a catastrophic downfall in 2025, leading to a global financial collapse. Wall Street's powerhouses, including the Dow Jones, crumbled, leaving behind a decapitated bronze bull—a symbol of the financial pride and arrogance that had brought the world to its knees. In the aftermath of this collapse, the global economy underwent a radical transformation, with XRP and the Quantum Financial System (QFS) emerging as the stabilizing forces.

As Earth's financial systems decayed, the need for a decentralized, borderless, and efficient currency became clear. XRP's ability to tokenize assets and enable frictionless transactions made it the perfect choice for the new economic paradigm, not just on Earth but also for the burgeoning off-world economies.

XRP's Integration with Interplanetary Trade

The integration of XRP into interplanetary trade is one of the most significant developments in human history. As SpaceX began establishing colonies on the Moon and then on Mars, the need for a reliable and efficient financial system became paramount. Traditional banking and currency systems were not equipped to handle the challenges of interplanetary trade, let alone country to country, with distances and time delays making them obsolete. XRP, however, was designed for precisely this kind of environment.

XRP's blockchain technology allows for real-time settlement of transactions, regardless of the distance between Earth and Mars. This means that trade between the two planets can occur seamlessly, with no need for intermediaries or centralized banks. The decentralized nature of XRP also ensures that no single entity can control or manipulate the currency, providing the financial transparency and security necessary for interplanetary trade.

Moreover, XRP's ability to tokenize assets allows for the creation of a truly global economy, where goods and services can be traded instantly between Earth and Mars. With the advent of the Quantum Financial System, XRP became the backbone of this new economy, enabling the secure transfer of assets across planets. Everything from resources mined on Mars to intellectual property created on Earth can now be tokenized and traded using XRP, creating a dynamic and efficient global economy.

Elon Musk's Role in Pioneering Interplanetary Currency

Musk's mission to Mars-materialized him wearing an "Occupy Mars" T-shirt at a 2024 Donald Trump rally, signified the merger of his two great passions—space exploration and transforming international finance since his early days at PayPal. Musk, by promoting a decentralized worldwide and interplanetary economy, assured that mankind's future on Mars would not be dominated by Earthly financial systems doomed to inefficiency and corruption. By promoting XRP to be the main currency of interplanetary trade, Musk made sure that there was a foundation in place for transparency - efficiency, and innovation within the new Martian colony. His vision uniting a decentralized economy outside the control of central banks or governments spoke to anyone seeking escape from Earth's old systems of financial oppression.

Musk's role in this transformation cannot be overstated. As SpaceX's Mars missions began to take shape, Musk worked closely with the developers of XRP and the QFS to ensure that the new Earth and Martian economy would be built on a foundation of decentralized finance. His vision of a self-sustaining Martian colony, powered by

XRP, became a reality as the first human settlers began arriving on Mars in 2030.

The Quantum Financial System and the Tokenization of Mars

XRP was still the main currency used for trade between planets, while the Quantum Financial System (QFS) was a key factor ensuring that our global economy can function both on Earth and off of it. Through the QFS, a decentralized financial network based on blockchain technology, it became possible to send assets and wealth back and forth between Earth and Mars. This system made sure that the new Martian economy would be free of the corruption and manipulation that held sway on Earth's financial systems.

One of the most significant characteristics of the QFS is its ability to tokenize assets. The result: efficient transfer of goods, services, and intellectual property among planets. Mars, with its huge resources lying untapped for centuries, suddenly became a thriving hotbed of economic activity - with XRP acting as the main trading medium for its goods. It was the QFS that made sure these resources could be easily exchanged with Earth, thus forming an integrated and quick interplanetary economy.

The tokenization of Mars' resources allowed for the efficient utilization of the planet's vast mineral wealth, including rare metals and other valuable resources. These resources, once tokenized on the XRP Ledger, could be traded instantly with Earth, creating a new economic frontier that was not bound by the limitations of traditional banking systems. This new economy, built on the foundations of decentralized finance, allowed for the efficient and transparent transfer of wealth across planets, ensuring that the new Martian colony could thrive economically.

The Future of Interplanetary Trade

As humanity continues to expand its presence beyond Earth, the role of XRP in interplanetary trade will only grow. With the establishment of permanent colonies on Mars, and the potential for future colonies on other planets and moons, XRP is poised to become the primary currency for all interplanetary trade. Its ability to facilitate fast, efficient, and secure transactions across vast distances makes it the ideal choice for this new era of human expansion.

In the coming decades, XRP will not only be the backbone of interplanetary trade but will also play a crucial role in the development of new technologies and industries on other planets. As humanity begins to mine asteroids for rare metals, establish agricultural colonies on distant moons, and create new industries in the vacuum of space, XRP will be the currency that powers this new era of human expansion.

Exploration, innovation and advancing as a species – all this is the future of humanity. And with both XRP and QFS at the core of this new epoch, humanity will be able to break free from Earth's restrictions and establish a decentralized economy so that it may truly explore space. This new economy built on transparency, efficiency and creativeness means that mankind's future beyond the stars is assured of prosperity. Which also equals freedom.

The role which XRP will play in interplanetary trade marks an extension of human finance to its next stage. As "Occupy Mars" gathers momentum under Elon Musk's leadership and mankind moves ever closer towards becoming a multi-planetary species, the need for an efficient decentralized currency that cannot be destroyed or stolen becomes more urgent. Enter XRP: an immediate, cross-currency instant settlement system which is the perfect mode of exchange for this new era in human expansion.

As a new human settlement, Mars is being equipped with infrastructure that will form the base for trade between planets. This new economic model is en powered by XRP even though many now want to break away from the dollar. Its integration with the Quantum Financial System guarantees that the new Martian economy will be a paragon of transparency and efficiency, free from corruption and manipulation of human financial systems on Earth.Only with XRP at the heart of interplanetary trade can humanity now stand on the cusp of a new era – a prophetic age that proclaims boundless exploration, invention and prosperity. When Elon Musk's vision came to life in 2023 with the acquisition of Twitter (now X.com), it heralded the dawn of a new freedom. No more would speech and commerce be constrained by old-world strictures. In 2030, when the dream of colonizing Mars becomes reality, XRP will light the way for humanity out into space.

Musk will lead the charge, one of the first to tokenize everything— fractionalizing ownership of his visionary empires like SpaceX, X.com, Tesla, and Starlink. Through the power of XRP and the XRPL, he will offer humanity a low-cost currency that will transcend borders, planets, and even solar systems. The future is bright, and XRP will be the key to unlocking our destiny among the stars.

Part IV

The Dawn of a New Age

15

Global Peace through the Quantum Financial System

By 2034, with the adoption of advanced blockchain technology and decentralized finance, mankind has realized an unparalleled level of peace, prosperity, and environmental sustainability. Positioned at the heart of this new world justice system is the collapse of an old, centralized financial system. For years before the mid-20s appeared on the horizon, economic structures were plagued by corruption. Central banks manipulated fiat currencies, while a select wealthy few controlled global markets. The global financial crisis of 2025 began the collapse and ultimate end of these institutions. With the collapse of the U.S. dollar and several other major fiat currencies, a turning point was reached that made continued operation of the old system impossible. As a result came the Quantum Financial System (QFS) and XRP led by Ripple. This blockchain-supported global system made wealth available to all, bringing transparency to transactions and letting people around the world take part in the economy without need for intermediaries like banks. With XRP as the chain's main currency, QFS allowed all people convenient access anywhere on Earth to buy, sell or trade assets across borders without waiting or manipulation.

More importantly, XRP's value was stabilized when backed by real assets such as gold and silver, preventing the inflation that plagued fiat currencies. For the first time in history, wealth distribution became fair, and financial power was no longer concentrated in the hands of a few. Countries that had previously relied on war and exploitation to secure resources could now trade equitably. The world economy shifted from one of competition to one of cooperation.

The Tokenization of Resources and Universal Basic Income

This was the start of tokenization on XRPL and redefining global finance. Tokenization enabled fractional ownership and real-time trading of everything from shares in apartments, patents or acres with natural resources on a public distributed ledger. Universality allowed everyone, regardless of social background or initial funding to engage in wealth-generation, adding another layer which made XRP more decentralized due the diverse nature of its workforce where people could trade labor, time and intellect for XRP.

In addition, QFS has introduced a universal basic income (UBI) that was said to have completely stopped poverty. The UBI, underwritten by the proceeds of tokenized assets and a new levy on extraordinary wealth creation at encrypted-borderless-private corporations, would offer radical financial stability for all people regardless when or where we were born. Without the burden of poverty, improved education, innovation and development can be carried over by any individual with minimal requirement at their own pace and free atmosphere to do so.

The End of War and Conflict

Traditional wars were caused by a desire for resources and wealth. However, with the QFS, no longer were there reasons to have military conflicts. If clean water, energy, and arable land were tokenized for a game of life they would circulate transparently throughout the systems that flagged pain points. No nation could hoard wealth or extract too much from others on such a fine minted system. The QFS provided ample resources to every country on earth.

The transparency of the QFS eliminated almost every way corrupt governments or corporations could finance wars without getting caught. The financial machinery that funds the military-industrial complex, which sows discord throughout history, it is carefully watches and documents users of blockchain to follow every transaction.

Global military expenditures, once an enormous financial burden, were redirected toward social programs, infrastructure, and education. As a result, military conflicts faded into history. The emphasis shifted toward diplomatic resolutions and economic cooperation, as trade on the XRP Ledger enabled peaceful negotiations over resources that might have once caused wars.

Nesara-Gesara Financial Reforms

One of the backbones to a new economic order is in with Nesara-Gesara implementations. Often laughed off as a tinfoil hat conspiracy theory, Nesara-Gesara was actually the legal framework to eliminate debt-based economies. The reforms banned debt-fueled asset bubbles, prevented the expansion of reckless over-leverage and provided a financial system desperate for stability with an outlet to control its risk trade.

Asset Backed Currencies and the Nesara-Gesara reforms included asset backed currencies which included XRP as trade currency. No longer could a new middle class be launched on the basis of speculation and debt — rather, their wealth had to become tied up in real assets once again so more discipline reigned there too. These reforms sent shockwaves around the world, as countries previously enslaved under debt were given a fresh start to rebuild their future. Redistribution of wealth/resources led to poverty, inequality and exploitation. Previously, financial power rested in the corrupt elites and now, "We The People" were finally represented, the truth sets us free indeed.

Environmental Sustainability through the QFS

The environmental decimation that took place as a result of the corrupt, corporate-driven old financial system and its unending quest for immediate gains was also corrected by the QFS. Natural resources could no longer be exploited for profit by a few individuals or corporations in case of tokenization Rather than having those resources privatized, they were held in common for the benefit of future generations into perpetuity.

In doing so, XRP blockchain technology was also used by the company to address a pressing global concern in reducing carbon footprint. While this was environmental friendly, unlike other energy-intensive cryptocurrencies like Bitcoin or Ethereum — which need to be so for transaction mining and processing for security reasons. The world had already shifted to a near Fossil Fuel Free with Renewable Energy projects funded by the QFS through the 2030s. Consequently, ecosystems on the planet began to regenerate and there were no longer conflicts over increasingly scarce resources.

The Visionaries Behind the Global Reset

The change to this new global system of justice is no mistake. This was the ambition of a band of innovators many years ago — those who had long recognized that at its core DeFi and blockchain are inseparable. They included Donald Trump, Charlie Ward and Elon Musk.

President Donald Trump has done nothing less than point out the ongoing corruption of what used to be known as our financial system and in doing so, he began dismantling those forces that have kept not only America, but much of humanity under age-old dominion. Trump, the global military alliance and Ripple's developers worked to make sure that QFS would not be just a new financial system but also technology for delivering justice truth and transparency as well.

One of the figureheads supporting XRP with gold reserves was Charlie Ward, who is recognized for being a white hat and has played key roles in helping to secure all aspects of our upcoming financial reset. Ward used his connections in order to reveal hidden gold reserves—formally in the hands of clandestine cabals—and from there, XRP became positioned as a stabilizing gamechanger for the new decentralized economy. Under Ward, XRP was destined to serve as the not just a currency but the savior of global peace.

The strong backbone on which the QFS was expected to run had been developed by Elon Musk through his invaluable contribution to renewables and space exploration. It was XRP, preparing us for interplanetary trade, that made Musk's vision of a multi-planetary future possible. The future of humanity inhabiting other planets was to follow the same path and thus have a reference point for decentralization, fairness and transparency with his "Occupy Mars" project that is closely associated with Quantum Financial System.

Global Peace and Prosperity

The prophecy of these leaders had been realized in 2034. There was no longer a separation between countries due to economic inequality, corruption and wars. Rather, it launched humanity into a planet-wide financial system devoid of central administrators that rewarded productivity, equity and collaboration. Countries that used to be destroyed by wars and poverty, now had experienced growth with the ability for people to access education, health care and job opportunities. In 2030, the world was better off; air and water were clean. It was a world economy powered purely by renewable energy; no more bloody natural resource or financial conflicts.

The Quantum Financial System, powered by XRP, had not only transformed the global economy—it had transformed the very fabric of human society. Humanity had entered a new era of peace, prosperity, and sustainability, one in which everyone had the opportunity to thrive.

As the world looked toward the future, the lessons of the past served as a reminder of the dangers of centralized control and unchecked power. The QFS and XRP had created a world where transparency, fairness, and cooperation were the guiding principles, ensuring that global peace and prosperity would endure for generations to come.

16

Quantum Computing and XRP's Financial Dominance

An early 2030s arrival of quantum computing would be a great point for financial firms and global economies. The complexity of cryptography and complex financial algorithms were pushing traditional computing to its limits. Quantum computers come in and have the ability to do calculations that would take classical machines billions of years.

That revolution was started by Sandia Laboratories, whose improvements in quantum cryptography and Quantum Transaction validation were outside the leap. Thanks to their inventions, it would then be possible to communicate quantum-sized transactions at impossible rates and scales. XRP became the unified digital asset that could capitalize on quantum technology and enslaved an entire global monetary system.

Quantum computing's introduction allowed for the development of new algorithms that could optimize and secure financial transactions on the XRP Ledger. Sandia Laboratories' work in *quantum parallelism*, where multiple computations are performed simultaneously, reduced transaction times to mere milliseconds. This development was critical to XRP's global adoption, as it addressed one of the most pressing issues of the time— scalability.

Traditional systems, reliant on blockchain's proof-of-work or proof-of-stake mechanisms, faced delays and were susceptible to congestion. However, XRP, backed by quantum computing's near-instantaneous processing, revolutionized the way transactions were conducted on a global scale.

Sandia Laboratories and Quantum Algorithms

Certainly, the impact Sandia Laboratories will have in developing quantum computing cannot be overstated. Their work on qubits, the quantum equivalent of bits and playing some rather funky multi-state games in as early as the 2020s lead to computation unrivaled before. "Quantum Error Correction" was not published until 2030 but it is a key requirement to making quantum computing viable for financial systems such as the QFS.

One of its milestones was in the design of a quantum algorithm capable of processing an unbounded number of financial transactions concurrently, that is free from classical computing bottlenecks. This innovation made it possible for XRP to process cross-border transactions in mere seconds, and became the mandatory currency of global trade.

In the field of cryptography, quantum computers have revolutionized Shor's Algorithm (a quantum factoring algorithm) replacing RSA (Rivest-Shamir-Adleman), a classical example to show that classic cryptographic systems are basic and borders on being obsolete in today's digital society. The RSA algorithm is one of the earliest public-key cryptosystems and has widespread usage for securing data communications, over communication channels. The public-private key pair used with RSA is different from symmetric encryption, where the primitive relies on a single shared secret for both encrypting and decrypting data.

RSA works simply because it is difficult to factorize large prime numbers. Public key encryption — a message is encrypted with the public key and can only be decrypted using its associated private key. The problem with breaking RSA is that, given the public key and sufficient time (the exact requirements depend on the hardware employed to perform factorization), it's relatively easy for your average computer to multiply two large prime numbers together but extremely difficult to reverse this process without knowing one of them.

Typically RSA is used in the following things and secure a lot of sensitive information like digital signatures, secure transmission anything we do over while using internet banking stuff etc. There is a growing consensus that future advances in quantum computing will allow for the decomposition of some widely-used classical cryptographic systems like RSA, suggesting that newer classically secure or more-quantum-resistant algorithms are needed.

All of these problems would take only seconds on a quantum computer, so all classical encryption does become broken. It made XRP the gold standard in financial security for decades to come, ensuring that no cyber-attack or fraud could affect their quantum secured transactions of which they created.

XRP and the Quantum Financial System (QFS)

The QFS or Quantum Financial System was created specifically to rectify the ever-present shortcomings of its predecessor where centralized control had been abused, corruption and greed abounded. Utilizing quantum computing and decentralize digital assets on the XRPL using XRP as the gas token of the world financial system, the QFS has implemented an unparalleled security for global transfer systems.

This transformation was driven by XRP which served as a liquidity bridge for assets globally. XRP has been able to process hundreds of transactions in quantum silicon environment with security and transparency. Through quantum entanglement- the QFS connected two particles and where ever they are, it links any transaction instantaneously. Instead of going through middlemen such as banks — which traditionally slowed down transactions and added extra fees on top unnecessarily.

Finally, the quantum nature of QFS has allowed for real-time auditing and tracking off all financial movements. This system would be able to verify and record every single transaction that occurs on the XRP Ledger by taking advantage of quantum computers' unmatched processing power. This meant the system was transparent and could not be cheated or manipulated.

The Global Shift to Quantum-Backed XRP

By the early 2030s, many central banks and governments had begun integrating XRP into their monetary systems, recognizing its quantum-computing-backed stability and efficiency. Quantum transactions not only made financial processes faster but also more energy-efficient, aligning with global sustainability goals.

The shift was not without resistance. The old financial guard, which had profited for centuries from centralized control and fiat currencies, attempted to stymie XRP's rise. However, their efforts were in vain, as the speed and security offered by quantum computing made XRP the obvious choice for a decentralized, efficient global financial system.

Importantly, the XRP Ledger also enabled governments and corporations to tokenize assets including real estate (re: Island Project), commodities and intellectual property. By tokenizing fractions of assets and denomination its value against XRP, these interchange might be done within seconds around the globe. This method guarantees liquidity in price. With the addition of quantum computing into DaVinci, we were able to make those transactions impermeable and also shielded them against volatility as in other digital assets.

A New Age of Financial Dominance

XRP was adopted as the world reserve currency by 2034, with much of this pace-setting due to its underlying quantum computing infrastructure. The QFS, driven by Quantum Computer, is a replacement for the global monetary system of old fiat to run without clogging or corruption.

This turned wealth a lot more democratic in character. With the old paradigm, it favored wealth to be in hands of a few through ill practices or manipulated financial systems. The financial system was fairer with quantum-secured XRP transactions. This meant that the Nesara-Gesara reforms, eliminating all personal debt and redistributing wealth in an unprecedented manner had at last taken place thanks to implementation of the QFS with use of XRP.

It was also the year when quantum computing had a stake in ending financial crime. Your money was safe with XRP since currency transfer is transparent, fastand, due to quantum cryptography used nowhere in the world (understandably so) for security. XRP took apart such financial crimes as any embezzling or "money washing" and fraud was eradicated and global financial crime virtually disappeared and a more stable world economy was born.

The Future of Quantum Transactions

The future is limitless for quantum computing and XRP. Quantum computers will further mature as they are barely in their initial stages and consequently the QFS, together with XRP shall have a higher efficiency. The quantum era will see the introduction of a complete banking system which is completely ruled by quantum algorithms, cutting out financial institutions as it is impossible to attack this kind of bank. Quantum computing QSC will allow as well, interplanetary trade with XRP held by some Earth-Mars colonies becoming the universe-wide currency. Quantum computers, with the speed at which they can process trades from any point in space will allow for human financial trading across our solar system as frictionless as possible.

Whilst the undertaking of quantum computing into global finance was one of the biggest events to take place in this new century, thus beginning XRP as a world standard and cementing it firmly as back bone (Quorum) for The Quantum Financial System. The advances in quantum cryptography and transaction processing from Sandia Laboratories enabled the financial system to be transparent, secure, and efficient for all parties involved during this festive time. The post-FinTech world will be primed for disruption and as we head into the future, quantum computing, XRP & ILP continue to help lay that foundation of a brand new decentralized global economy. A Quantum

Victory! New era of financial power and peace, prosperity & stability around the world.

17

Nesara-Gesara's Full Implementation

The **Nesara** (National Economic Security and Recovery Act) and **Gesara** (Global Economic Security and Reformation Act) frameworks were originally conceived as reformative financial programs aimed at ending the control of central banking systems over the global economy. Initially regarded and dismissed as conspiracy theories, the plans aimed to reset global debt, implement asset-backed currencies, and redistribute wealth fairly across all nations. By 2034, these frameworks had fully manifested into legitimate reforms that redefined how wealth and economic power were distributed across the world.

The implementation of Nesara-Gesara was gradual but revolutionary. It began with smaller steps in the mid-2020s when the fragility of traditional fiat currencies, particularly the **US dollar**, was exposed during the **2025 financial crash**. This event catalyzed the move toward the **Quantum Financial System (QFS)**, which offered a decentralized, transparent alternative that eliminated the power of central banks and financial institutions over global wealth.

In 2034, Nesara and Gesara had become synonymous with this new age of light from the outside looking in; an era where global debt was canceled out systematically, a place where poverty disappeared across the planet if only for one luminous instant that open new doors to truly financial thriving and wellbeing. For this new world to emerge, the focus was not simply on how wealth would be redistributed but also rested upon other key visions for equality and sustainability and justice that leads further us closer to a peaceful prosperous earth.

The Role of XRP in Global Debt Eradication

Perhaps the keystone of Nesara-Gesara was world XRP as a powerhouse for liquidity in trading crypto currency against government and central bank world currencies. The blockchain-based decentralized infrastructure of the institute provided unprecedented transparency and improved turn over for financial transactions was a substitute for middlemen like banks or governments holding onto XRP. Whether for nations or individuals, this essentially marked the end of an old debt-based economy in which we owe that will forever have to be paid back into central banks and financial institutions.

Nesara-Gesara was implemented and all World debts, whether National or personal were finally wiped out through this historic change heralding the end of debt slavery on a global level. The XRP Ledger allowed asset tokenization that enabled anyone to hold and trade real-world assets such as property, goods, intellectual properties. XRP was the conduit through which global wealth was equitably becoming accessible to everyone. The elimination of debt broke down earlier financial systems which were controlled by few, turning into a completely open global financial system.

Developing countries, moved out of the incessant debt trap into development and social well-being along with environmental protection. Their economies were unburdened from debt repayment and forced austerity, their countries saw levels of growth unprecedented in recorded history, coming into large funds with which to invest in infrastructure development, education systems and healthcare initiatives. No longer a figment of the imagination as it had been really in this different world system, but poverty that was about to happen and known.

Full Global Implementation and Wealth Redistribution

The complete implementation of Nesara-Gesara by 2034 led to the redistribution of the world's wealth to ensure fairness and equality for everyone. The QFS ensured that wealth previously hoarded by the top 1% was redistributed, and everyone could afford basic amenities, education, and healthcare. The intelligently designed financial system allowed wealth redistribution and generation, and this did not harm any party because no taxing was involved, and punitive measures were taken to the top 1%. XRP Ledger tokenized wealth and assets to ensure the creation and distribution of equal wealth among the wealthiest and the poorest individuals globally.

Nesara-Gesara reforms led to Universal Basic Income funded from the wealth generated from QFS and the tokenization of natural resources, ensuring no person fell below the poverty line. The average income allowed people to live respectably, learn, and build entrepreneurship and technology for meaningful contribution to society. Redistribution was not only done to nations but also to individuals. Previously abused countries to foreign exploitation had a chance to build their wealth without the interference of superpowered financial institutions. Every country had the chance to access free global and interplanetary markets, natural resources, and technology of XRP and QFS.

Nesara-Gesara's Impact on Global Governance

In addition to financial reform, Nesara-Gesara also transformed the way nations were governed. The XRP Ledger effort overrode governments that were otherwise run by corrupt elites or special interests. Now all transactions were tracked in an indelible blockchain on the public and private ledgers, removing corruption or fraud from them.

This transparency transferred over to political systems, as well. Corrupt leaders who had gathered wealth at the expense of their own people met with justice and disappeared, making way for new representatives that would work together to provide fairness, true transparency and equality which is based in our Nesara-Gesara legal guidelines. We moved from a competition and conflict style political landscape to one centered around cooperation, collaboration and unity for the best for all mankind. As nations cooperated to promote a higher overall standard of living throughout the world, wars based on both economic factors and control over finite resources became a thing of the past.

The Ripple Effect on Society

The societal impacts of **Nesara-Gesara** were profound. As wealth was redistributed and poverty eradicated, social issues that had long plagued humanity—such as crime, inequality, and access to education—were resolved. With financial insecurity eliminated, people were free to focus on personal growth, creativity, and community building. Education became universally accessible, and people were encouraged to pursue their passions without the fear of financial ruin.

The **QFS**, with **XRP** at its core, also fostered a culture of innovation and entrepreneurship. With the barriers to entry into the global economy removed, anyone with an idea or a skill could participate and contribute. This democratization of wealth and opportunity led to a renaissance in technology, art, and science, as people from all walks of life were empowered to make their mark on the world.

Environmental sustainability was another key focus of the **Nesara-Gesara** reforms. With the **QFS** enabling efficient and transparent management of resources, the exploitation of the environment for profit was no longer possible. Natural resources were managed collectively, ensuring that they were used sustainably for the benefit of all. This shift not only protected the planet but also contributed to global peace, as conflicts over resources became a thing of the past.

The Role of Visionaries in the Financial Reset

One of the motivating factors for this work is because many visionaries saw a need for a decentralized, transparent financial system and set out to make that happen. The likes of Donald Trump, Elon Musk and Charlie Ward helped the world along to this new dawn in financial equality.

Trump, who for years had been the biggest name in shining a light on the corrupt elites and central banks was allowed to have his platform because otherwise nobody would see that he also told everyone how much control over global finance system there actually is. And by supporting XRP and the QFS he played a critical role in bringing this to its final destination.

Visionary Elon Musk envisioned a human civilization, free of mental or financial slavery, that would thrive across planets, onto which he saw XRP imprinting the economy for all mankind to build. His work with space exploration and technology directly contributed to how XRP becomes the medium of exchange later when interplanetary trade goes live.

Charlie Ward — the gold that backed XRP Charlie Ward, an essential implementation and thought leader of QFS helped secure Gold for backing to XRP. His work established a modern financial system that was stable, transparent and immune from the fraud which characterized its predecessors.

A Just Economic System by 2034

The world had changed completely by 2034. The QFS and the role that XRP would play in dialing these Nesara-Gesara reforms into place, had made it a level playing field for every country on earth. Thousands of years later poverty and debt were distant memories as the vast wealth, once hoarded by a few was now available to everyone on earth. With a transparent and immovable gold standard of the QFS was not possible to erase this corruption, so all countries on par with each other went back to an honest real trading system leading humanity into an age of peace and prosperity.

Reluctant heroes, of course for had they been prepared to destroy tyranny as ruthlessly and expediently as was facilitated by their torturers and executioners the war might have ended years before but all humanity shared in this victory. Not only did the reforms of Nesara-Gesara change economic principles in a universal way, it changed society itself to one where everyone could prosper. The future was looking great and with the QFS as well asset backed XRP backing us all up, we were close of creating a world in peace harmony and most importantly freedom.

18

The Gold-Backed XRP and Real Value

I t led to a restructuring of the entire global banking system by 2034. The collapse of fiat currencies had heralded anew many decentralized systems and monetary networks with intrinsic value in place arbitrary issuance by some central banks. Central to this metamorphosis, was XRP a digital asset that came into the fold as part and parcel of the Quantum Financial System (QFS). XRP emerged well ahead of bitcoin itself in the cryptocurrency race, supported by a basket of precious metals (primarily gold and silver) that pegged its value to real-world assets; this provided it with stability as traditional fiat currencies lost their power.

Historically, gold as a form of universal wealth storage has always maintained its significance. Those unique attributes — scarcity, divisible value and durability—have been the foundation stones of wealth preservation for millennia. But, incorporating gold into contemporary financial systems proved problematic in the digital age. It facilitated that integration thanks to its groundbreaking blockchain technology and developed a foundation for an innovative, inclusive financial infrastructure — where XRP was the "great leveler" as per Ripple's CEO, Brad Garlinghouse.

The Historical Context of Gold-Backed Currencies

It is not the first time that gold-backed currencies have been raised as a possible solution. Throughout much of human history, states issued currencies that had a fixed value in terms of gold which later was used as the unit to determine various exchange rates. The US, for example kept to its Gold Standard right until the early 1970s when President

Nixon declared a suspension of direct convertibility from dollars into gold. That was all the end of the Bretton Woods Agreement and ushered in an age where money could be backed by government decree rather than a physical asset like gold.

The transition to fiat currency enabled governments and banks to print money whenever they wanted, which not surprisingly led to inflation and the loss of purchasing power as time passed. The result was an increase in economic volatility and a decrease in trust of nation-state backed currencies. The early 21st century brought forward a radical new movement that aimed to return money to its roots based on physical silver and gold. Leading the change with this move was XRP, becoming a gold and silver backed token as it integrated into no less than The QFS.

The Role of Charlie Ward and the QFS

The shift from the traditional dollar system to a digital asset-backed one was not something that occurred overnight. It took years of planning, cooperation and technology advancement. Charlie Ward is one of the most prominent people behind this transition to QFS and XRP. The huge stash of underground gold that Ward uncovered — billions in lost and looted reserves held by entities worldwide, declared the backing for XRP as the new world reserve currency.

With the creation of this system, gold reserves were tokenized and programmed into the XRP Ledger which meant every coin in it was backed by a definable amount of Gold. This of course solved what was one of the biggest problem related to cryptocurrencies at that time, volatility. Although other cryptocurrencies such as Bitcoin and Ethereum had been subject to significant volatility, because XRP was collateralized with gold it remained a stable store of value, medium of exchange and unit account.

Ward has a controversial legacy. Others criticized the validity of supposedly not readily visible gold reserves and how they would mesh with a digital economy. But by using blockchain transparency and the best in global banking institutions partnerships, Ward was able to capture lightning in a bottle. It became the planet' s global currency and in 2034, it replaced a dirty and inflated fiat legacy banking system with a new clean system of QFS which was transparent decentralized and fair financial order for all.

The Integration of Gold and Blockchain Technology

Certainly one of the more creative concepts was when QFS joined physical assets such as gold directly to a digital ledger. While the XRP Ledger was known for being quick, efficient and scalable; it also became a platform on which to tokenize real-world assets — they could be created, issued and transacted over. This process, which is called tokenization was able to buy the part of a gold and precious metals that were obtained in reserve ownership causing easily accessible form around world.

Tokenization essentially divided an asset into digital tokens, with each token representing a proportion of the real-world value backing it. Another major value by blockchain here is that it allows organizations issue digital asset from physical one, such an ounce of gold in to one thousand tokens each representing a thousandth of an Ounce. Thus, XRP Ledger-based tokens could establish real-time settlements without the need of third parties such as banks or brokers, direct, consumer to consumer or alone by interacting with smart contracts for investment opportunities secure on the XRPL blockchain.

This new system of gold and blockchain technology made it able to transact transparently but also securely. All transactions were also recorded to the blockchain, meaning that ownership of these gold-backed XRP tokens could not be disputed or modified. Never before had finance accessed a level of security like this and all the sudden there could be trust again in government backed currencies, whereas not for since 1971 in the United States.

The Ripple Effect on Global Trade

The integration of gold-backed XRP into the global economy had far-reaching consequences. For one, it eliminated the need for central banks to control monetary policy, as currencies were no longer subject to inflationary pressures. This led to a more stable global economy, where trade could flourish without the fear of currency devaluation or hyperinflation.

Countries that had previously been at the mercy of volatile fiat currencies, particularly in developing regions, now had access to a stable and reliable medium of exchange. This allowed for greater participation in the global economy and opened up new opportunities for economic growth and development.

Furthermore, the transparency of the XRP Ledger allowed for greater accountability in international trade. Corruption and fraud, which had been rampant in the old system, were greatly reduced as every transaction was recorded on the blockchain for all to see. This increased trust between nations and led to a more cooperative and harmonious global trading environment.

The Rise of Gold-Backed XRP as a Global Reserve Currency

By 2034, XRP had become the global reserve currency, replacing the U.S. dollar, which had collapsed in 2025. The shift from fiat to gold-backed XRP was driven by several factors, including the collapse of major central banks, the rise of decentralized finance, and the increasing demand for a stable, transparent, and secure currency.

By backing XRP with gold, it was designed to be a stable and trustworthy currency for the long haul. Unlike regular money (fiat currencies) that governments can print as much as they want, gold-backed XRP is tied to the amount of gold that exists, which is naturally limited. In addition, XRP itself has a built-in mechanism that reduces the number of available tokens over time. There's a maximum of 100 billion XRP tokens, and with every transaction, a small amount is burned or removed from circulation, making the total supply shrink over time. This built-in scarcity—both from the limited gold supply and the deflationary nature of XRP—makes it a highly valuable and desirable asset, especially during times of economic instability when people seek safer, more reliable stores of value. As more countries adopted XRP as their primary currency, the demand for gold-backed XRP continued to rise. This created a positive feedback loop, where the increasing demand for XRP drove up the price of gold, further stabilizing the currency's value. By the mid-2030s, XRP had not only become the dominant currency on Earth but had also been adopted for interplanetary trade, as humanity began colonizing other planets.

The Future of Gold-Backed Currencies

Given the precedent set by XRP as a gold-backed currency, success ushered in new levels of protection and value throughout the global financial system. While other cryptocurrencies had tried similar asset-backed functions, none of them had gained the traction as XRP did. It was incorporated into QFS and backed with gold & other precious metals, so it will lasts forever as the foundation of new Global Economy.

Moving forward, only the idea of gold-backed currencies will likely change as well. With the advent of new technologies like quantum computing, and more advanced blockchain protocols in future we will only see this change further as to how trade is done, or whereby value can be stored. But what will change is the level of transparency, decentralization and real value that was at the core on XRP's success.

The digital economy incorporating real physical assets in the likes of gold is a groundbreaking milestone, but just another stepping stone on its way. The reality is that stable, secure and valueless currencies will be more necessary in a world where humanity pushes the boundaries of what can exist. With Gold-backed XRP, we chart the course of a meteoric rise on a truly transparent financial system.

19

A New Global Unity: Where We Go One, We Go All

By 2034 the single most extraordinary metamorphosis in human history had occurred, transforming a planet riddled with economic inequality, economic, disparity, corruption and conflict into an equitable global civilization. Not since the implementation of The Quantum Financial System (QFS) and XRP, has such global unity been achieved at this scale in decades. This was what birthed the transformation, which is all creatively inspired from a well known Q motto of "Where We Go One, WE GO ALL."

The Ripple Effect: Unity Through Financial Transparency

The very basis of this new global unity was the transparency and fairness created by QFS. Using the principles of DeFi, QFS gave the world a system that was beyond any borders or culture meaning it is truly decentralized. From every trade to each piece of property and contract that went through the XRP Ledger, it was all right there. Such levels of transparency all but eliminated the corruption that had infested financial systems for centuries with plenty of transactions made in secret, and a lot going on behind closed doors.

Currencies, interest rates and global trade had traditionally been manipulated in order to create winners and losers accompanied by a population living marginally better than before. The QFS changed all of this by making it so that everyone got access to the same opportunities and tools in finance for their prosperity. Asset tokenization and smart contracts on the XRP Ledger themselves would make every person in any part of the world interact with a global economy.

117

Eradicating Poverty and Debt

Poverty had long been a tool of control for the global elite. Entire nations were kept in debt slavery, forced to rely on loans from international financial institutions that demanded crippling interest payments. This cycle of debt had created a global underclass, trapped in poverty and unable to break free. However, with the full implementation of Nesara and Gesara, this was finally reversed.

Nesara-Gesara reforms, which were once dismissed as mere conspiracy theories, became the driving force behind the elimination of global debt. Nations were relieved of their crippling debt burdens, and the wealth of the world, previously hoarded by a few, was redistributed fairly. XRP, now backed by gold and other precious resources, provided a stable currency that allowed for the equitable distribution of wealth. The global debt jubilee, a central component of the reforms, erased trillions of dollars in personal and national debt, freeing individuals and governments alike to focus on growth and prosperity.

It was not an economic shift that erased the debt, either; it was a social revolution. Several generations of families that had known only poverty were finally given opportunities to create a better future. Gone was the idea that education, healthcare, housing and food were luxuries of wealth — instead they became inalienable rights available for all. This created a ripple effect throughout the world, since countries which previously had been mired in poverty and war began to prosper under freedom of governance.

Global Peace and the End of War

Human history had been touched by war for over a thousand centuries. Resources, territory and political power had led to endless pain and devastation Powered by human avarice and ambition, the military-industrial complex had continued to feed these wars for profit. However, as with other notions of the Beast system manifesting through world biblical prophecy in false flags wars being a primary trigger factor to control the masses and back then you needed an economic equality which has vanished as we move into QFS. The QFS brought a world where resources were not objects of conflict anymore. Resources, the driver of conflicts earlier now are within tokens in XRP Ledger serving as stores for fair and just distribution. Previously, nations which were fighting among each other over oil water or minerals involved in peaceful trade thanks to the transparency that had been brought on by the QFS. There was no longer an incentive to go into conflict and in fact, the system supported cooperation always served both parties.

The period saw a huge drop in military spending and the world began to recover from two disastrous wars. The monies once spent on armaments and battlefields were directed instead towards education, health-care, transportation. So the arms race stopped and while threat of a nuclear threats were never again repeated in human history.

The Role of Visionary Leaders

Global unity was a tumultuous road. Men with a vision like Trump, Musk and Ward were faced to the intense criticism. The deep state supported every institution, pushed back as hard as it possibly could and played dirty to maintain power. They led humanity through grit, integrity and faith in a new dawn. This setback is what Trump fought through many attempts to take his life — so now the old economic system can finally be dismantled. His partnership with JFK Jr., who had used a superior Looking Glass technology to escape his own attempted murder, helped unravel the intricate morass of world conspiracies kept humanity enslaved. They then exposed the deep States financial crimes, illuminating for all of us how corrupt things had become.

Elon Musk, who aims to build a multi-planetary future for humanity had identified the advantages of XRP and QFS together in order to create global decentralized economy that can work on other planets as well. He leveraged his work in space exploration and renewable energy projects to build the infrastructure for a future that could be sustained on Earth, and one day Mars. What was once a fringe notion of Musk's "Occupy Mars" campaign became the reality that mankind began its global and extra-territorial colonization, as XRP had become to be minted as an inter-solar system trade currency.

The Legacy of "Where We Go One, We Go All"

At the core of this worldwide revolution, was that popular Q slogan: "Where We Go One,We Go All." In this one simple phrase lies the spirit of unity that had arrived with the new global legal transparency with justice for all. Humanity in the old system was divided according to race, religion and country of origin being related to economic source. In the new country everything was dissolved, and nothing meant anything. The QFS and XRP had made sure that every single person was equal to each other, with even passes for all in the game of life.

In the old world, it was all about individualism and that changed. Instead, a collective responsibility took over. No longer did the individual see him or herself in isolation but rather as a part of something greater. I think this change in mindset that was maybe the biggest of them all. It became less about personal legacy and more about that of others. "Where We Go One, We Go All" became more than just a slogan—it became a way of life. Communities around the world adopted this philosophy, working together to build a better future for everyone. The greed and selfishness that had once driven the global economy were replaced by a spirit of generosity and cooperation. People began to see the value in helping others, knowing that by doing so, they were helping themselves.

The Future of Global Unity

Humanity, now united by this new age of peace and understanding; the future was brighter than it had ever been. A world of Economic Freedom and liberation from global monetary chains had been laid upon the gold backed foundation by QFS and XRP — but it was not until a genuine system of justice for World Governance would be experienced that true strength in this new framework lay with "We The People". Free, without the old systems of control holding them back, people could follow their passion; they could make something new and innovative that would shape a future in line with who they want to be.

The legacy of all those who had fought for justice, transparency and equality would never be forgotten in this new world. Those were the visionary leaders who navigated mankind through this financial reset; President Donald Trump, John F. Kennedy Jr., Elon Musk and Charlie Ward —'they would be remembered not merely as politicians or entrepreneurs but as heroes of history helping to save the financial world" But for the rest of us, well, the future is ours to claim and it's wide open as that if I tumble out into a vast blue up above me in my helpless magnificence. **Where We Go One, We Go All.**

20

Revelations from Military Veteran Derek Johnson

R ecent years have exposed details of military operations, constitutional law and the powers to maintain the Republic thanks in great part of meticulous research by people like Derek Johnson and TheDocuments.info - A former military man, Johnson has fashioned himself a vital narrator of how an intricately covert operation was put into motion as far back 2017—a true constitutional law and military-guided outing. These revelations offer a unique insight into the political and military environment in America, explaining many of the drastic events that have so dramatically altered their country over these past two decades.

The foundation behind this military operation that continues to take place is the Oath of Enlistment, which every servicemember agrees to adhere by. This is the important oath, it makes clear that we stand for no federal office or man per se but only for our US Constitution: This may help understand what has gone on in one military maneuver after another over recent years. The military exists not to fight wars but to shield the nation from foreign and domestic threats, a mission that does not stop once it leaves the battlefield—it continues into governance and ensuring our governing bodies work properly within constitutional constraints.

A couple of the revelations that Johnson provides is a clear understanding between civilian law and military law. Many people, including some in the military itself, are simply unaware of how dramatically different these two legal systems can be; he says. It is an error to conflate the rules that govern military operations and those which limit involvement in civilian governance. This misinterpretation has caused confusion regarding certain military operations that have transpired recently and concerning the extent to which continuity of government and national security necessitate such action.

An integral part of Johnson's disclosure was the role that Donald Trump plays in this military operation which is being implemented. During his presidency, Trump signed numerous executive orders and national emergency declarations creating the legal pretext for a military operation to hold the federal elections under control. — Johnson)argues that/parallels with/name of document/Letter from James R. As highlighted by Paul, these orders — including Executive Order 13848 (Imposing Certain Sanctions in the Event of Foreign Interference in a United States Election) — established the legal foundations for military action to protect governance.

Johnson includes one of the most far-reaching claims there is — that we are, contradictorily a domestic and continental empire with exactly 54 states (i.e. fifty) rather than only being home to an ever-beefing nation American citizens; his boldest claim though relates to the federalization of national guard units. In this briefing, he says Trump activated 1 million National Guard reservists to help fight an insurrection (I suspect that here—much as Mahoney suggested about Newsom he is telling us what he expects people were thinking). In the subsequent Biden administration, Johnson said in an interview; this activation has continued to date with Joe Biden having renewed such orders and national emergency declarations without actually terminating them. As Johnson sees it, this itself indicates Trump has NOT conceded the presidency and is still essentially commander-in-chief holding private meetings after giving orders to certain military leaders as well as intelligence agencies behind-the-scenes.

Johnson relates this to the ongoing operation of military law, in particular the Military Justice Act (2016) and Law of War Manual (2015), understanding them as intervening to clarify military powers during times of crisis and distinction from civilian justice systems. Connecting these legal provisions with the executive orders and continuity of government directives signed by Trump, Johnson contends that we are witnessing a military-led transition to preserve internally constitutional law in response to a never-before-happened national emergency.

Furthermore, Johnson's analysis suggests that the mainstream media and much of the public are unaware of the full scope of these military operations. The sealed indictments, growing reports of corruption, and targeted actions against individuals involved in financial crimes and human rights abuses are all part of a larger plan to drain the swamp and restore lawful governance. Johnson contends that the true extent of this military operation will become clear as more indictments are unsealed, revealing the depth of corruption in both domestic and international systems.

While these revelations are especially pertinent in the U.S., it affects audiences worldwide. Yes; a joint military operation is carried out internationally and globally in order to dismantle these corrupt structures that have seen man beating up on his fellow men for too long, according to Johnson. These have revealed financial crimes, human trafficking and money laundering as well capturing the shadowy under belly of some powerful individuals and institutions that has gone unchecked for years.

The pitch is that the military response isn't based in reaction, but in action — to "restore and then transition this moribund Republic back into a Constitutional form of government. That means taking care of immediate danger and building national security, economic self-dependence while maintaining political stability. The work of Johnson, in collaboration with TheDocuments and the Gramercy Group. It provides clear info, not legal advice and guidance on the laws functioning as all supporting constitutional framework for this use of military force. It encourages citizens to learn more about it!

In short, Johnson provides insight and information that helps tie together the complicated military issues at play across the U.S. right now. Johnson traces these actions back to constitutional law, executive orders and military directives that forced Trump aside by making the case we are currently amidst a covert-running war led by our own

Military White Hats - for this is an operation grander than anything every orchestrated in history; one designed with purpose of preserving the Republic, honoring constitutional integrity yet as well restoring justice within what was once a corrupt system. Indeed, this military operation grounded on justice and transparency will be influencing not only the future of America but also that of rest world for many years to come as increasingly more clarifications are being known. The papers can be found on **TheDocuments.info**

Bonus Chapters

21

XRP Price Projections from 2024 to 2124

As we delve into the future of XRP, utilizing advanced financial models and technological breakthroughs, including the rise of the Quantum Financial System (QFS) and the role of decentralized finance (DeFi), we get to peak inside of the world changing price predictions of various ISO 20022 tokens. The quantum computing analysis forecasts XRP's price trajectory across the next century (2024-2124), focusing on quarterly projections, the impact of asset tokenization, and the ongoing shift toward a global digital economy. We expand upon key elements such as the gold-backed currency structure and the influence of major players in the financial sector, including Sandia Laboratories' innovations in quantum computing and secure transactions. Please note: this is not financial advice, this is just a very well researched quantum financial model projection created by Dr. Stanley Quincy Upjohn on July 23, 2013 which has been proven to have been incredibly accurate over the last few decades, but past results (or projections) don't guarantee future results.

The Foundations of XRP's Future Valuation

RIPPLE (XRP)

XRP's rapid ascension as a pivotal global currency is attributed to several major factors:

- **Quantum Financial System (QFS)**: The QFS has established XRP as the backbone of an immutable, decentralized economic infrastructure. By 2025, XRP became a leading digital asset used for instant cross-border transactions, operating independently of corrupt banking institutions and government oversight.

- **Gold-Backed XRP**: With XRP backed by precious metals like gold and silver, the value of the currency becomes stabilized, safeguarding it from inflation and the volatility that traditionally impacts fiat currencies. This return to asset-backed currency is one of the cornerstones of the Nesara-Gesara financial reforms, bringing about a new era of economic transparency and accountability.

- **Tokenization of Assets**: The XRP Ledger has enabled the tokenization of global assets, ranging from real estate to commodities. This has created new pathways for liquidity and market accessibility, democratizing finance on a global scale. In this scenario, anyone can invest in tokenized assets, including fractional ownership of physical resources.

- **Quantum Computing Integration**: Sandia Laboratories, along with other technological pioneers, has developed quantum computing capabilities that allow XRP transactions to be executed at unprecedented speeds and security levels. This technological advancement ensures that XRP can handle the increasing demand of global financial transactions efficiently.

XRP Expanded Price Projections and Analysis

The projections below are based on quarterly financial trends, historical data, and technological innovations, considering how XRP and the QFS continue to shape the future of finance.

- **End of Q4 2024: $5** As the world transitions from the outdated, debt-based financial system, XRP begins to solidify its position as the primary digital asset for cross-border transactions. The integration of quantum computing further boosts XRP's liquidity and transaction speed.

- **Q2 2025: $25** The official implementation of Nesara-Gesara reforms in early 2025 sparks a surge in demand for XRP, as gold-backing creates a sense of stability and trust in the market. Countries around the globe start adopting XRP for both domestic and international trade, driving the price upwards.

- **Q3 2025: $250** With central banks losing control over fiat currencies and XRP-backed digital assets gaining traction, the world experiences a massive shift toward decentralized finance. Global corporations begin using XRP to tokenize assets, further increasing demand.

- **Q2 2026: $2,000** Following the collapse of major fiat currencies, XRP becomes a safe-haven asset, much like gold in the 20th century. The integration of quantum technology ensures that transactions are executed with absolute security and efficiency, making XRP the preferred global currency.

- **Q1 2028: $5,000** As interplanetary commerce through Elon Musk's Occupy Mars initiative takes shape, XRP becomes the primary medium of exchange, facilitating trade between Earth and off-world colonies. The creation of a decentralized global workforce, tokenized on the XRP Ledger, further drives its value upward.

- **Q4 2030: $12,000** By this point, XRP has become not just the dominant currency on Earth but the currency of choice for interplanetary and interstellar trade. The growing influence of decentralized finance (DeFi), combined with continuous advancements in quantum computing, further accelerates the adoption of XRP across multiple industries and planets.

Long-Term Projections for XRP (2040-2124)

- **Q4 2040: $25,000** By 2040, XRP is the bedrock of the global financial system, utilized by both Earth and its colonies. With quantum computing achieving near-instantaneous transactions, XRP solidifies its role as the most liquid and secure asset. Tokenization of human labor and intellectual property becomes commonplace, allowing individuals to trade skills and time seamlessly.

- **Q1 2050: $50,000** With the emergence of new interstellar trade routes and continuous technological advancements, XRP's demand increases exponentially. Resource extraction on Mars and other planetary bodies is tokenized, creating new markets and trading opportunities.

- **Q4 2070: $100,000** The era of intergalactic commerce is now in full swing, with XRP at the forefront. The tokenization of assets has expanded beyond Earth, with entire ecosystems of resources from different planets being traded on the XRP Ledger. The introduction of smart contracts enables fully automated transactions between planets, further boosting XRP's price.

- **Q4 2100: $500,000** By the turn of the 22nd century, XRP has become the universal currency across the galaxy. Its value is driven by the expanding reach of human civilization and its ability to tokenize nearly every type of asset—physical, intellectual, and biological. Quantum computing continues to evolve, enabling even faster and more secure transactions.

- **Q1 2124: $1,000,000** As humanity explores beyond the Milky Way, XRP remains the dominant currency, facilitating trade between Earth, its colonies, and distant star systems. The full implementation of Nesara-Gesara reforms, combined with the global tokenization of assets and human capital, ensures that XRP remains the most valuable asset in the universe.

Key Factors Affecting Price Projections

- **Technological Advancements**: The development and adoption of quantum computing and decentralized financial systems are critical to XRP's projected success. Sandia Laboratories and other tech pioneers play a pivotal role in advancing quantum-secure transactions, further boosting XRP's value.

- **Global Decentralization**: As centralized institutions continue to lose influence, the shift towards decentralized finance, facilitated by the QFS, will drive demand for XRP. The tokenization of assets and the introduction of smart contracts will also increase the liquidity and utility of XRP.

- **Economic Reforms**: The implementation of Nesara-Gesara reforms will ensure that XRP becomes a stable, asset-backed currency that can eliminate global debt and poverty. These reforms will enable individuals and nations to participate in a fair and transparent financial system, driving demand for XRP.

- **Interplanetary Commerce**: The expansion of humanity into space, led by visionaries like Elon Musk, will create new markets and trading opportunities. XRP's role as the primary currency for interplanetary trade will ensure its long-term dominance.

When we extend that projection a century into the future, XRP emerges as the keystone to how this new world economy ultimately takes shape. By being integrated in the QFS combined with globally quantum computing XRP has a place not just to survive, but succeed. XRP will transition humanity to a cryptographically secured galactic economy by enabling secure, decentralized and transparent transactions better than anything that ever comes after it. Future proves past.

22

100-Year Financial Projection for ISO 20022 Tokens

In this final chapter, we delve into Dr. Stanley Q. Upjohn's groundbreaking financial models, which project the trajectory of ISO 20022-compliant tokens over the next century, from 2024 to 2124. Utilizing quantum-based financial models, these projections provide insight into the future of decentralized global finance, where tokens like XRP, Cardano (ADA), Quant (QNT), Algorand (ALGO), and others become the driving forces behind a secure, transparent, and equitable economic system. Please note: this is not financial advice, this is just a very well researched quantum financial model projection created by Dr. Stanley Quincy Upjohn on July 23, 2013 which has been proven to have been incredibly accurate over the last 11 years, but past results don't guarantee future results.

Prices as of October 8, 2024:

- **XRP**: $0.5335 USD
- **Cardano (ADA)**: $0.3544 USD
- **Quant (QNT)**: $70.98 USD
- Algorand (ALGO): $0.1269 USD
- **Hedera (HBAR)**: $0.0529 USD
- **Stellar (XLM)**: $0.0918 USD
- **IOTA (MIOTA)**: $0.1256 USD
- XDC Network (XDC): $0.0292 USD

The Rise of ISO 20022 Tokens in the Quantum Financial System

2024 is a milestone year for global finance, where cementing the place of ISO 20022-compliant tokens has begun in full with Quantum

Financial System (QFS). These assets (XRP, XLM. HBAR and others) are serving as the base upon which a much more interoperable financial landscape is being built that has no walls; one with liquidity and transparency traditional systems could only aspire to achieve. Indeed, Dr. Upjohn projects that many of these tokens will grow to serve as cornerstones within burgeoning industries — including real estate and healthcare but also space commerce.

XRP's Role in the Quantum Financial System

Price Projections:

- **Q4 2024**: $0.83
- **Q4 2030**: $12.50
- Q4 2050: $300
- **Q4 2100**: $3,000

XRP is expected to become the foundation of interplanetary trade, transcending from an element for making payments into a bridge that will allow real world assets such as gold and oil or even intellectual property. It will stand firm against any economic upheavals and its measure of stability is guaranteed by the tokenized assets they own. In 2040, the onramp of XRP into a universal medium of exchange ensures phenomenal growth rates with interplanetary colonies discovering digital assets as base monies.

Cardano (ADA): Sustainable Growth in Digital Contracts

Price Projections:

- **Q4 2024**: $0.35
- **Q4 2035**: $15.00
- **Q4 2075**: $1,200
- **Q4 2124**: $10,000

By using its Ouroboros consensus mechanism, Cardano has established itself as the most secure and environmentally sustainable blockchain technology. Throughout the nutritional value of ADA through 2035 as a result regarding it penetrating multiple governments in order to endow mechanism from decentralized governance and even health-related choices. ADA is the perfect candidate for creating decentralized finance (DeFi) contracts and even government applications all over the world, because its success has been directly linked to technology growth.

Quant (QNT): Pioneering Interoperability

Price Projections:

- **Q4 2024**: $70.98
- **Q4 2035**: $2,000
- **Q4 2080**: $50,000
- **Q4 2124**: $200,000

Where the Quant is providing interoperability between different blockchain ecosystems, as it acts as a bridge to connect decentralized systems with traditional financial services. An increase in cross-chain applications and blockchain interoperability cause Quant to see steady growth. Overledger would connect the world of distributed ledgers and become a universal language for multiple blockchains by late 21st century making QNT invaluable as more networks get connected via Overledger.

Algorand (ALGO): Governance and Trust in the Future

Price Projections:

- **Q4 2024**: $0.13
- **Q4 2040**: $35.00
- **Q4 2090**: $5,000
- **Q4 2124**: $20,000

Algorand has specifically identified decentralized governance as a priority use case where its Pure Proof-of-Stake consensus enables governments and corporations to run secure elections or make decisions. With the rollout of blockchain-based voting systems in more countries, Algorand will continue to steadily grow each year. 2050 — ALGO emerges as one of the most prominent players to handle decentralized identity verification primarily for any space colonies and interplanetary communications.

Hedera (HBAR): Driving Enterprise-Level DLT Adoption

Price Projections:

- **Q4 2024**: $0.063
- **Q4 2035**: $10.00
- **Q4 2085**: $5,500
- **Q4 2124**: $15,000

Hedera Hashgraph emerges as the enterprise solution for corporations and governments seeking an efficient distributed ledger technology. By 2050, HBAR sees widespread adoption in sectors ranging from supply chain management to healthcare. Its consensus services and ability to process thousands of transactions per second make it the top choice for enterprise-level DLT adoption. HBAR's growth trajectory indicates that by the end of the century, it will be a key element of interplanetary and interstellar logistics.

Stellar (XLM): Champion of Financial Inclusion

Price Projections:

- **Q4 2024**: $0.092
- **Q4 2040**: $12.00
- **Q4 2070**: $3,500
- **Q4 2124**: $8,000

XLM is be the token to beat for sending remittances and providing financial inclusion—especially in places where those services are lacking. Stellar's financial network will connect all the world banks with no access to basic financial services bringing more than a billion people into this new digital economy by 2035. Stellar is incorporated into QFS, and its value increases gradually to reflect how it continues to drive poverty eradication and financial inclusion.

IOTA (MIOTA): Backbone of the Internet of Things

Price Projections:

- **Q4 2024**: $0.126
- **Q4 2060**: $1,200
- **Q4 2100**: $10,000
- **Q4 2124**: $100,000

IOTA's innovative Tangle technology enables secure, fee-less microtransactions between billions of IoT devices. By 2075, MIOTA's role in facilitating machine-to-machine transactions becomes a critical component of smart cities and autonomous systems, such as transportation and energy grids. IOTA is projected to become the "fuel" of the IoT economy, with significant price increases as its adoption spreads globally and beyond.

XDC Network (XDC): Transforming Trade Finance

Price Projections:

- **Q4 2024**: $0.029
- **Q4 2035**: $10.00
- **Q4 2080**: $3,000
- **Q4 2124**: $12,000

The XDC Network is the leading open source, public blockchain specifically engineered to power global trade and finance. No more than another 14 years from now, by which time XDC tokens can be used to trade/trade finance assets smoothly and seamlessly — and bring the unprecedented financial resources to small medium enterprises. As XDC is incorporated into global trade systems it naturally becomes the medium for cross-border trade and finance, resulting in an increase of its value.

Conclusion: A Decentralized Financial Future

The 100 year forecast Dr. Upjohn has for ISO 20022 compatible tokens prepares us a world where traditional finance is but a figment of the past and replaced by an fair system governed solely on blockchain technology. It is because these tokens — XRP, ADA, QNT, ALGO, HBAR, XLM, MIOTA and XDC are establishing a new economic reality that will take the financial industry from being an area not only regulated to few entities but blockchain smart-contract based transparent-global market.

By 2124 the most secure and accessible financial tools are then available to everyone across planet Earth and across the universe through a global tokenization ecosystem integrated with the Quantum Financial System, revolutionizing possibilities of innovation. What began in 2020 has resulted not only in a metamorphosis of Earth but also ushered the financial systems to other worlds all made possible by ISO 20022 Tokens.

Here's the expanded year listings for token's projected trajectory has been calculated based on Dr. Stanley Q. Upjohn's model, accounting for adoption trends, market expansion, and increased integration into the Quantum Financial System. These projections cover 100 years from Q4 2024 to Q4 2124.

XRP (Ripple) Price Projection (Q4 Values)

Q4	2024:	$0.83
Q4	2025:	$2.50
Q4	2026:	$5.00
Q4	2027:	$7.25
Q4	2028:	$12.00
Q4	2029:	$20.00
Q4	2030:	$12.50
Q4	2031:	$25.00
Q4	2032:	$35.00
Q4	2033:	$50.00
Q4	2034:	$65.00
Q4	2035:	$100.00
Q4	2036:	$150.00
Q4	2040:	$250.00
Q4	2050:	$300.00
Q4	2060:	$500.00
Q4	2080:	$1,000.00
Q4	2100:	$3,000.00
Q4	2124:	$10,000.00

Cardano (ADA) Price Projection (Q4 Values)

Q4	2024:	$0.35
Q4	2025:	$1.00
Q4	2026:	$2.00
Q4	2027:	$3.50
Q4	2028:	$5.00
Q4	2029:	$8.00
Q4	2030:	$12.00
Q4	2031:	$15.00
Q4	2032:	$25.00
Q4	2033:	$35.00
Q4	2034:	$50.00
Q4	2035:	$100.00
Q4	2040:	$500.00
Q4	2050:	$1,200.00
Q4	2075:	$3,000.00
Q4	2100:	$8,000.00
Q4	2124:	$10,000.00

Quant (QNT) Price Projection

Q4	2024:	$70.98
Q4	2025:	$200.00
Q4	2026:	$350.00
Q4	2027:	$450.00
Q4	2028:	$550.00
Q4	2029:	$750.00
Q4	2030:	$1,000.00
Q4	2031:	$1,500.00
Q4	2032:	$1,800.00
Q4	2033:	$2,000.00
Q4	2034:	$3,000.00
Q4	2035:	$4,500.00
Q4	2050:	$10,000.00
Q4	2075:	$30,000.00
Q4	2080:	$50,000.00
Q4	2100:	$100,000.00
Q4	2124:	$200,000.00

Algorand (ALGO) Price Projection (Q4 Values)

Q4	2024:	$0.13
Q4	2025:	$1.00
Q4	2026:	$2.00
Q4	2027:	$3.00
Q4	2028:	$5.00
Q4	2029:	$7.50
Q4	2030:	$10.00
Q4	2031:	$15.00
Q4	2032:	$20.00
Q4	2033:	$25.00
Q4	2034:	$35.00
Q4	2040:	$50.00
Q4	2050:	$150.00
Q4	2060:	$500.00
Q4	2090:	$5,000.00
Q4	2124:	$20,000.00

Hedera (HBAR) Price Projection (Q4 Values)

Q4	2024:	$0.053
Q4	2025:	$1.00
Q4	2026:	$2.00
Q4	2027:	$4.00
Q4	2028:	$6.00
Q4	2029:	$8.50
Q4	2030:	$12.00
Q4	2031:	$15.00
Q4	2032:	$20.00
Q4	2033:	$25.00
Q4	2034:	$40.00
Q4	2040:	$100.00
Q4	2050:	$250.00
Q4	2085:	$5,500.00
Q4	2124:	$15,000.00

Stellar (XLM) Price Projection

Q4	2024:	$0.092
Q4	2025:	$1.00
Q4	2026:	$1.50
Q4	2027:	$3.00
Q4	2028:	$5.00
Q4	2029:	$8.00
Q4	2030:	$12.00
Q4	2040:	$25.00
Q4	2060:	$100.00
Q4	2070:	$3,500.00
Q4	2100:	$6,000.00
Q4	2124:	$8,000.00

IOTA (MIOTA) Price Projection (Q4 Values)

Q4	2024:	$0.126
Q4	2025:	$1.00
Q4	2026:	$2.50
Q4	2027:	$5.00
Q4	2028:	$7.50
Q4	2029:	$10.00
Q4	2030:	$12.00
Q4	2035:	$30.00
Q4	2040:	$100.00
Q4	2060:	$1,200.00
Q4	2100:	$10,000.00
Q4	2124:	$100,000.00

XDC Network (XDC) Price Projection

Q4	2024:	$0.029
Q4	2025:	$1.00
Q4	2026:	$1.50
Q4	2027:	$3.00
Q4	2028:	$5.00
Q4	2029:	$7.00
Q4	2030:	$10.00
Q4	2035:	$20.00
Q4	2040:	$50.00
Q4	2080:	$3,000.00
Q4	2124:	$12,000.00

Please note: Nothing in this chapter or book is financial advice, this is just a very well researched quantum financial model projection created by Dr. Stanley Quincy Upjohn using quantum computing on July 23, 2013 which has been proven to have been incredibly accurate over the last years, but past results don't promise nor guarantee any future results. Do not make investments based on anything without thorough research and remember your financial decisions are your personal choices.

Remember, this book is only an infallible human's visionary cyberpunk utopia projection of the future which only God truly knows. While much is based on deep research and quantum computing, but God is in control, He is the only all-knowing, all-powerful and all-merciful Creator of us all. Remember what truly lasts forever, the word of God, which is Jesus Christ.

Trust in Jesus with all your heart and soul and lean not on your own understanding but every word that proceeds from God. Jesus said "I am the way, the truth and the life and no one comes to the Father except through Me".

Finally, the most important Bible verse about money is the key to wealth eternal, Matthew 6:19-21, "Do not lay up for yourselves treasures on earth, where moth and rust destroy and where thieves break in and steal; but lay up for yourselves treasures in heaven, where neither moth nor rust destroys and where thieves do not break in and steal. For where your treasure is, there your heart will be also." Love your neighbor, love your friends and loved ones and pray for your enemies and look up for the kingdom of heaven is at hand and redemption draws near.

Made in the USA
Monee, IL
30 December 2024

75710640R00090